The Psychic
& Spiritual
Awareness Manual

A guide to DIY enlightment

T0159446

The Psychic
& Spiritual
Awareness Manual

A guide to DIY enlightment

Kevin West

Winchester, UK
Washington, USA

First published by Sixth Books, 2014
Sixth Books is an imprint of John Hunt Publishing Ltd., Laurel House, Station Approach,
Alresford, Hants, SO24 9JH, UK
office1@jhpbooks.net
www.johnhuntpublishing.com
www.6th-books.com

For distributor details and how to order please visit the 'Ordering' section on our website.

ISBN: 978 1 78279 397 7

A CIP catalogue record for this book is available from the British Library.

Design: Lee Nash

Printed and bound by CPI Group (UK) Ltd, Croydon, CR0 4YY

We operate a distinctive and ethical publishing philosophy in all
areas of our business, from our global network of authors to
production and worldwide distribution.

CONTENTS

Preface

We may be forgiven for thinking of ourselves as human beings who sometimes have spiritual experiences. I believe, as do Native Americans, that we are spiritual beings who sometimes have human experiences. We are each born to a unique path, understanding and determination in life; travelling a road signed with psychic and spiritual awareness. However, it would appear that a small but significant number seem determined to keep us from fully realising this, and much more. Add to that the dominance of a culture of greed and reliance on material things that characterises and pervades in the modern era, and you have a perfect recipe for the divorce of heaven from earth and the toxic separation of mind, body and spirit. But friends, this is not the way of things!

Many so-called teachers and exponents misrepresent what is a common ability within us all by wrapping it in a fake mystique and bogus etiquette. Time for change! As the former president of one of the best provincial institutions for Spiritualism in England, I promise you the message carried forth in this work will help you realign and better connect you with your natural Divinity. There is no reason why you cannot understand and even *do* all the works contained herein and greater.

Although this is in no way a complete volume, it is hoped it will serve to inspire students and teachers alike into a deeper thinking about the nature of our being. It finds its veracity in the sizeable amount of work I have undertaken since 1983 to the present as a master in (what I call) 'Natural' Spiritualism and Gnostic disciplines. This is inclusive of being a president, spiritual medium, healer and teacher. To this end I have taken some of the best teachings and awareness classes delivered by some of the finest instructors and exponents over the years throughout England and Wales and incorporated them into these easy to follow exercises subdivided into chapters. You are warmly invited to fill in the gaps with your own special and unique experiences.

This book is both a message and a diagnostic tool. I sincerely hope it makes you want to go out and try these things for yourself either by starting your own group or seeking out similar. It will also help you to become more critical of much of what is on offer in the esoteric world. Learn the principles of what is in here and you will become an accomplished exponent: balanced in mentality, physicality and spirit.

Chapter One

The Vessel

So you want to know how to develop your psychic sensitivity and your spiritual awareness? Perhaps you have had experiences throughout your life that have taught you there is far more to heaven and earth than meets the eye. Maybe you have watched certain people on TV, read about in them books, saw them at theatres, psychic and spiritual centres demonstrating amazing talents. Do you think to yourself, 'If only I could do that. I wish I was that gifted'? Well you are. Every human soul contains these abilities; the problem is how to access and use them and that is what this book is really all about. We are already possessed of these talents from birth, but the unguided, the uninitiated and the feebleminded can easily find themselves foiled attempting to understand it. Knowing the path and walking it are two completely different things! Books can teach you much but will *do* nothing for you any more than a repair manual will operate the machine it describes. A play may be written down, but it is a lifeless thing until it is produced, directed and performed to a real and responsive audience.

To get into the right frame, it may help if we think of ourselves as vessels and instruments. These are good visual basics to describe how we work. The vessel implies you are ready to be filled and the instrument implies you are ready to be used.

Although we shall occasionally use the term, strictly speaking, there is no such thing as a 'gift'. For a gift implies something for nothing. All those who tread this path have the following in common. They will be able to count amongst their qualities, compassion, love, charity, faith and oneness. A musician is born with a certain ability to play, but it is only when the musician becomes trained and disciplined that they discover the endless possibilities of their skill. Not everyone can be a musician, but we all know how to tap our feet, listen and perhaps hum a tune. In much the same way, not everyone can be a medium, but we all have our sensitive moments when we see beyond the veil of human life. It is true to say that people have different abilities. Some have it stronger than others and some have talents across a range. This book is about helping you realise *your* potential: *your* abilities. If the edict that one is taught in accordance to one's ability to learn is true, then the good student will be willing to persevere through all the categories of this work in order to acquire a basic working knowledge of each discipline cited.

It is an enjoyable journey, usually requiring the worker in the field to have suffered many frustrations and difficulties often beyond the understanding of those around them. By way of remedy, this new journey will reinvest the enquirer with dignity, self-assurance and the quiet confidence to become an active, not passive, participant in their own world. Along the way you will achieve, if you have not already, a black belt in mental karate. It is an enjoyable trek, entirely in your own hands – no one else's! There is no quick fix scheme when it comes to the journey of the soul; only a fool would say otherwise.

Chapter Two

Earth, the School of Learning

There is a school we all attend no matter what colour, class or creed we may be. It is a school where you progress by your own efforts and not off the backs of others. It is a school without a shortcut or fast track to learning. This school is called the earth from which the only graduation is the death of the physical body. The good student need master only one simple lesson – you are responsible for everything you do. Once you realise this then you have cracked it! Further, that when you are doing or thinking bad then you are harming yourself the most. The effect of this is multiplied many times if you apply it to harming others.

As you sew, so shall you reap. As you do, so you are. As you think, so shall you become. People often fail to understand this, confusing it with a karmic principle. In reality nothing could be simpler. To reap what you sew should be self-evident. The second part means you are what you do. So if you do bad things then that is what you are. The thought aspect can find its reliability in, let us say, the physical structure of your home was someone's idea, was it not? They had the thought and built the house. Their thought became the reality. Take St Paul's Cathedral in London for instance. Sir Christopher Wren had an idea for how a new cathedral might look. He then set about designing every nook, cranny and façade. His thought became the reality. Ergo, as you think, so shall *you* become. Think only the best of yourself and it will happen.

In your life you will have suffered many terrible things. Fear not for you are in good company. It is the way of life on earth and recognising it is half the battle in dealing with it. The crime is in letting this suffering negatively shape and affect your spiritual outlook on life. Sensitive as you are, do not be like those who

3

allow bad experience to cloud their judgment and spill over into everyday conversation, action and thought. Ultimately they have revenge in their hearts. Instead, use the great past masters of light as your examples. Be like those who walk this path with their faces clean and smiling and their hearts filled with love and compassion. And as for being put upon, usurped, overlooked and condemned by others, let not these things awaken the tigers of revenge in you, but instead, awaken the dove of peace that these terrible things should hold life with you no more. If you can take on these ideas then already you are well on the path to progress. Your unique spiritual development will be meaningless unless you, the vessel, have the aforementioned qualities. But before we go any further there is another compound hurdle to tackle – that of piety, image and the giving out of a false impression about oneself to others in order to cultivate an air of mystique, or worse still, a pedestal upon which to put oneself. In spiritual centres, churches, temples, workshops, classes and organisations, how often do we see people with titles, teaching, giving advice, demonstrating and working, who love nothing more than to be seen of others doing the same? Remember, psychic and spiritual awareness does not mean piety. If it did then we would be awash with saints. There are many healers, mediums and so on, who are far from saintly – *never forget that.*

It is said that the gifts of the spirit manifest the world over in all sorts of ways. Take many of the great writers, poets, artists and composers who have transcribed the works of the spirit to the earth. Very few, if any of them, could be described as saints or, prophets. So too with the abilities of the worker in the vineyards of the spirit world. Some of the most spiritually aware people to have walked the earth were also known to have killed. It shows us that spirit and psychic power is like water – it flows wherever and whenever there are channels, men and women so constituted that this natural energy will flow freely through them. It is when we claim it as *our own* that we fall short of the *gift.* Remember, we are instruments and vessels only! Can the piano claim the credit for Mozart?

All too often people chastise themselves saying they are not worthy or good enough to do the work. You have nothing to lose but your chains. Just wanting to help others is the highest form of devotion you can make to your fellow humans. The prisons and courtrooms of the earth are filled with misjudged righteous people. And in pubs and bars you will find more spiritual people than you will in temples and churches. So, if that is your disposition then you are in the company of Ghandi, Jesus, Moses, Mohammed, Buddha, Viracocha and all the misinterpreted past masters of light who have gone before us. Now let us begin...

Chapter Three

Meditation: The Key to Communication

Communication with yourself, then with others

So what do we mean by meditation? Perhaps we could define meditation by suggesting it is to *reflect deeply upon*. Let us focus on two main types, *passive* and *active*. Passive means that whilst you are meditating you may not necessarily be controlling what is happening to you or what you are receiving. You are, in a sense, sitting and listening; a kind of observer to what is going on – a bit like a passenger in a car on a journey. *Active* can mean that you are meditating or reflecting on a specific thing for a specific outcome – a *driver* of the car if you like. Visualisation can have a big part to play, but if visualisation is something you find hard or impossible to do then there is an addendum to this section to help you.

So what are visualisations and what do teachers mean when they use this term? Visualisations are images generated, controlled and or used by you, the student. There is no great mystery or secret to visualisation, it is what we do every day when we remember, when we reflect, when we think or when we look at an old photograph. Have you noticed how with a photograph all the other related images come flooding back? To take this further, if you were asked to think of your front door you would have no difficulty. If you were then asked to describe it in detail, you would have no difficulty. You would see every blemish, every mark and every aspect, and while you did so, you would become almost absentminded as to your surroundings temporarily.

How do I open up? It simply requires from you, imagination and visualisation. What do I imagine? What do I visualise? There is no hard and fast rule to this, you simply visualise and imagine whatever you feel comfortable with and after all it is your meditation, your development and your opening up! A few helpful examples follow. But first of all, make your meditation a regular thing. This can mean once a day, once every other day, once a week, once a fortnight or once a month. Your meditation should seldom if ever be longer than one hour. Often just ten minutes a session can be quite sufficient.

EXERCISE
Remember, the less physical distractions the better. Sit as comfortable as possible to reduce fidget. To open up with, a few examples follow. Imagine one of the following:

- the petals on a beautiful or favourite flower opening up
- a beautiful deep sun slowly coming up over the horizon
- a door or gateway of light slowly opening before you
- a speck of light slowly growing in strength, vibrancy and colour
- or your own opening prayer

Begin to take normal, relaxed, controlled breaths. You may even visualise colours that you feel or may have been told are harmonic to your development. If you have a knowledge or awareness of chakras, you may like to work with these; however, *control* and *responsibility* are well-advised by-words where these seven sacred petalled points are concerned. Misuse of them can open you up to all sorts of stress, fatigue and energy exhaustion. Ignorance of them will not preclude your development and once you are ready, these will open automatically.

If you wish to reflect on a particular subject then you should send out special thoughts throughout that particular day or prior to the particular time of your meditation. The way spirit will work with you is directly proportional to the discipline you hold!

This is common sense. For instance, at the start of your meditation you may find that you are too pre-occupied with the events of the day; such earthly things as your mortgage, your work, family problems, things on your mind that are unique to you and so on. Don't worry, this is a perfectly normal thing to happen. Just let these things come into your psyche – let them flood in and bother you. The vessel, that is you, needs to begin to empty before the pure spirit can enter. After a while these things will stop and soon give way to the higher self: the purer thought vibration from within you (the real and often unexplored you). Remember too, your elder brothers and sisters are there with you, right by your side, every step of the way, calling upon you to do better each time.

Before we begin any kind of development, we ask for only the highest and the best from the other side of life. At the novice stage, make sure you ask for divine protection (Chapter Sixteen). After opening up with a visual such as those aforementioned, imagine then a bubble around yourself extending approximately 40cm from your body. With practice this ability becomes easier. You are, in effect, energising your spirit aura. As stated in Chapter Five, this is the aura that extends furthest from the body. When you are comfortable with this, ask your doorkeeper/ guardian angel to step in (this is not a blood relative or friend you have known). These are special spirit people who work with you all the days of your earthly life. Feel their presence. Get to know them. Feel the special power and love that they bring. They will never desert you and will always protect you. It does not matter if you are unaware of their identity: gender, culture or indeed anything concrete about them. The important thing at this stage is to simply feel their presence and know that they are there with you.

After a time you may want to move on to something a little more involved. If this is the case then here are some helpful hints.

Focus on one or more of the following:

- A loved one and the special memories you have shared.
- A guide, a helper, a doorkeeper, your guardian angel.
- Entering a beautiful spiritual garden and wandering around. In this garden there is a lovely home or temple or building that surprises you. Go in and explore. Who or what is there?
- A walk along a beautiful coastline.

Always enjoy your meditations; they are walks with the etheric ones. Be nosey! When you are ready to finish you should always close down in reverse of the way in which you opened up, otherwise you risk remaining 'open'. This can be detrimental to your mental and emotional state and may display a lack of discipline on your part.

Heightened sensitivity is something ALL novices must be aware of. It is something that never goes away. You simply need to know how to deal with it. Failure to close down properly will make you susceptible to this condition. Its symptoms are many and varied and none of them good. These can include an inability to sleep, sensitivity to noise and conversation, irritation, a feeling of grogginess and an inability to relax. You may also pick up on a lot of the ambient negativity connected to certain types of people, situations and places. It is a problem that requires thorough understanding on your part in order to develop your special abilities to higher and further stages of spiritual awareness and application. So if you used any of the previous suggested methods with which to open up, simply close with one of the following:

- Close the petals on a beautiful flower.
- Watch a beautiful sun dip slowly beneath the horizon.
- See a door or gateway of light close slowly behind you.

- Observe a body of light diminishing in strength, vibrancy and colour.
- Recite a special closing prayer or one of your own.

Remember always to thank our etheric friends for their power, guidance and love. But first and foremost, always give thanks to the god of your choice *over* your guides, spirit friends and helpers. After all, when you pass over to the other side, they will be the first to say, 'Why did you pray to me? Why did you thank me? It is by the grace of the creator that we do what we do!'

Remember, as with any new skill, it requires dedication, patience and practice! The passive and active aspects of this class of meditation are easy to understand. Sometimes we lead, other times we are led. It is as simple as that. No worker ever developed his or her awareness without some degree of meditative contemplation or practice. It is only through meditation that we can still the anxieties of the conscious mind and let go the true self.

The late spiritual medium and teacher, Norma Meagher wrote,

Visions are what we meet on the meditation road and should not be lightly undertaken. It is very important to learn in the early stages, control of mind. That is why in the very first stages of approach to meditation, it is necessary to apply the mind sincerely to the lessons, for the deeper one goes into meditation, the more essential it becomes to have full control of the mind. This can only come about by applying concentration to each lesson. It will bring its own rewards when meditation is mastered. There are several planes of meditation, each one being deeper than the previous and each one bringing more knowledge. Control of the mind is necessary. Each plane inter-laps the other and the etheric becomes more flexible as each plane is reached. It is because of this flexibility that it is vital to have complete control of the mind. If we cannot control our mind, then we cannot control our wanderings. If we are to commune with knowledgeable beings, then we must learn how to allow the mind to take in knowledge correctly, lesson by lesson on each journey that it takes during meditation. Retention of knowledge is one of the things that have to be learned. It is true to say that each meditation brings its own reward that grows with each lesson to final fulfilment.

Meditation brings a calmness of mind, a serenity, a tranquillity that enables one to cope with everyday stresses and strains. Anger and frustration will lessen, whilst an inner glow will prevail. The ability to see clearer clairvoyantly will deepen gradually as will perception sharpen to a clearer sense of clarity. It will be very easy to put the mind to a higher plane, even during waking hours; especially so when anger or anxiety is present. Let me say here that meditation also develops the Healing gift to further stages. Meditation has the power to bring about Healing and Mediumship almost the instant it is needed. This is because, while meditation is deepening with every lesson you are also learning to contact and be at one with the higher spheres. True mediumship is the one that can reach out and transport itself into the spheres of light. It is here where you meet these intelligences and recognise them when they come to you. You will know them for sure, not only by their faces but by the Grace that surrounds them and the power they bring. It is all too easy to either sense or see something at your side and believe what they say, for they can take on many guises. Once you have walked and talked with them in their own sphere, you can never be fooled by false or lesser entities who profess to be what they are not!

Chapter Four

Crystal Tuning and Meditation

It is said the crystal picks you and not you, it!

Occurring naturally in the earth's crust, crystals are usually found one mile beneath the surface. There are various kinds, far too many to itemise here, but from ancient times they have held a constant fascination for people who are spiritually and psychically aware. They can be an aid to meditation, clairvoyance and many other disciplines. Uncut crystals, that are ethically mined, are said to have the greatest potential. Machined or exploded-from-the-ground samples are considered to be less effective by virtue of their violent extraction.

You must tune your crystal for the specific purpose required such as healing, meditation, clairvoyance to name but a few. Another rule is *one discipline – one crystal*. If you have a collection of crystals, it is said to be a good idea to group them together so they can recharge and feed each other. However, exponents of psychometry may disagree and view crystal contact in this manner as a contamination (see Chapter Eleven). For all that, it must be remembered that crystals are simply tools. Exposure of crystal to direct sunlight is a desirable way of energising them, and besides, they seldom look better than when bathed in the sun's rays.

For the purposes of this exercise we will be dealing with what we shall term our *special* crystals. Vibrations (levels of consciousness) are extremely important and having once acquired the crystal you must allow no one else to touch it. This may at first sound strange, but many times in the awareness class, where contamination has occurred, information from the reader to the recipient has ended up with the contaminant.

Should your crystal be cross-contaminated in any way then do not worry. There is a simple procedure for re-cleansing it again. Run it under a cold tap for at least two minutes. This will neutralise any undesired influence upon it. Always keep your crystals clean.

EXERCISE

Hold the crystal in your hands. Think of where it has come from – one or more miles beneath your feet. Think of the forces manifested in its creation and how it was formed from volcanic, molten rock, some of which may be over a billion years old. Look for a point or focus for the crystal; they all have one. Now examine the crystal carefully. Your eye is like a camera. Take some time to look at each feature and build up a mental picture of it for recall. Observe how parts of it may resemble a mini landscape – a mini world into which you can immerse yourself. See its surface as a new world to explore. The jagged fractal formations fascinate you. Distinguish what nature has made evident. Allow your brain to decode its shape and form like a new horizon of perception.

Now close your eyes and feel the crystal in your palms and with your fingertips. Build a tactile picture of it in your mind. Feel its vibration and energy in your hands.

Now hold the crystal to your stomach or solar plexus. Visualise the crystal remotely, say, a yard in front of you. Slowly, in your mind's eye, zoom towards the crystal, closer and closer until it appears as big as a castle. Now begin to fly over it, through its valleys, peaks and over its planes of intricate and fascinating detail. Reveal facets and features you never thought it had. And whilst you are doing this, you are looking for a way in. Take your time and take pleasure and benefit from this exercise – enjoy this feeling! It gets better and more rewarding with practice.

Eventually you locate an entrance. Enter therein. You are now across the threshold of an inner space within the crystal filled with light and joy. This secret interior can be big and cavernous, as wide as a beautiful beach or as small as a cosy room with a glowing fire; whichever you feel is best for you. The important thing is you are safe here. This is *your* space and no one can enter in save by your grace.

Now is the time to decide the purpose of the crystal. Is it for healing, meditation, clairvoyance, philosophy or some other discipline? If so, then think of this now! Program the crystal for one thing only. For example, you may see this as a meeting place for loved ones, guides, helpers and so forth. Invite them to join you here. It is also a space where you can ask questions and endeavour to receive answers and enjoy the surprise of receiving them. Dwell here a while, charging and recharging your world weary batteries. Come here when you are in *any* mood. Places of sanctuary are not for the sole reason of melancholia. Note too that at each stage you will be able to feel your vibration change and attune to be at one with the crystal you hold – your *special* crystal, which can embrace unlimited amounts of information.

When you are ready to come out, simply retrace your steps back out of the interior, out through the gateway and away from the crystal proper. Slowly zoom out to where the crystal appeared some feet away from you and open your eyes when ready. Now your crystal is tuned. Meditate with it anytime.

About Crystals

Crystals are considered as 'life' by many authorities. They are possessed of an innate structure which is incorruptible. When damaged, they can heal themselves. In spite of there being many types of crystals, they all fall into six categories. They form an integral part of modern day communications, from the old crystal radio sets to the silicon of the microchip processor. IBM's Marcel Vogel discovered they could be reprogrammed (and by the human mind) and used as chips for storing multi-terabytes of information. Approximately twenty-five per cent of the earth's crust is made of silicon. So marvel not that these have been used since time immemorial by ancient and illumined ones to access realms and facets of human consciousness we are only now rediscovering.

Chapter Five

Discerning Auras and Their Energies

Invisible fields of energy that surround all living things

Before we can discern the auras and their energies, we need to define what they are, what form they take and what each one does.

THE DIVINE SPARK is first, though not technically, an aura. It is the soul of the individual and creates all the auras and energies we see. It is the eternal spark contained within each of us. That divine spark is *you*. It sits at the centre of the prehistoric brain and is only millimetres in diameter.

THE MENTAL AND EMOTIONAL AURA emanates as a nimbus around the head only. Through practice and development it is possible to read and interpret these emanations in order to gather information on the sitter. This aura contains details about the sitter's mental and emotional states and how each affects their physical health. Early Christian art displays a transparent orb around the heads of certain illumined ones. Perhaps the artists may have seen it for real. The mental part has a further unique feature: a band over the top of the head from ear to ear and, like all the auras, is comprised of a prism of colours.

THE PHYSICAL AURA, ASTRAL OR SPIRIT BODY is the spirit counterpart and blueprint of the physical body. It is the vehicle we use when we astral travel and gives indication of past physical health conditions and disorders as well as current ones. It is the aura seen by clairvoyants when a loved one returns from the other side. It is how we recognise them. Sometimes spirits will return displaying infirmities or will appear old and frail, but this is simply a form of communication to show how they looked during their earthly life. The spirit body is without illness, blemish or disease and ceases to age when the human counterpart reaches early to mid-thirties.

THE SPIRITUAL AURA extends furthest from the body, usually one foot or so away. A good indication of this aura's influence can be found when someone invades our space. For instance, we may be on a bus or train or in an office and someone will sit too close. We may or may not feel comfortable with this invasion of our space. If there is a clash in the over lapping field the energies will distort, become resistant and will resemble something akin to the interference on a TV picture. If we are happy with this overlap, then a harmonic resonance may be perceived. By sensing this aura, we get a good indication as to the spiritual nature of the individual. It is said that so-called charismatic people have a strongly developed and widely expanded spirit aura. There are those who can change the atmosphere of a room or place as soon as they walk in by virtue of this aura's hidden energy and power to influence.

ENERGIES AND PSYCHIC IMPRINTS can be left on all things. People often wonder how an ancient object, stone or crystal can be read using psychometry (Chapter Eleven). Energy cannot be destroyed. If you take a piece of wood and burn it, you only change its form. The heat, the flames, the light, the smoke, the noise and ash are the sum of the original piece of wood you started out with. In other words, energy is transferable. It is the same with psychic energies. How often do we enter a room or house and feel or sense an atmosphere? These are latent psychic energies and emotions left in the space by events past and present that appear not to deteriorate with time.

EXERCISE

How to Discern the Auras

A good starting place is with your own aura. That may sound impossible to you at this stage but if you follow these teachings you will find impossible things redefined to you as very possible. As with any of the disciplines, you will need to find a quiet prepared space, sit comfortably and place the palms of your hands together at your solar plexus with fingers pointing away from you in what we will call 1st position. Draw your hands apart one inch and hold for anything up to a minute. In this position you are experiencing the physical aura, astral or spirit body. From one inch draw them apart four inches and hold them there for twenty seconds. Then bring them back together to one inch apart and hold. Do this several times and you will feel an invisible resistance, perhaps magnetic or like squeezing a balloon. Your next target is to draw them to twelve inches apart and hold and then bring them back to the 1st position, an inch apart and hold for twenty seconds. Do this several times, each time increasing the gap between your hands until they extend a full three feet apart to what we shall call 2nd position. At this distance you may experience the energy as a bar that your hands are compressing and expanding. You are now in the area of the spirit aura, but we shall address that in a moment. For now, with your palms this distance apart, turn them in towards your eyes. Now close your eyes and slowly, over a period of at least three minutes, bring your palms up to cover your eyes in what we will call 3rd position, but do *not* touch the head! As you begin to draw your hands up, a change in the aura field and the energies should be perceptible. This can be quite overwhelming. Stop when your hands are no closer than three inches from your face. Here you will feel another energy field. This is the mental and emotion aura surrounding the head, almost like a goldfish bowl. Sense its strength. Gently bounce your hands to amplify the feeling. At leisure and in your own time, have fun slowly exploring this aura by moving your hands around its nimbus. When you are done, bring your hands back over your eyes to where you started at 3rd position. From there, slowly draw your hands away to 2nd position where they were at three feet apart but with palms turned inwards opposing. In this position, you are once again at the limit of the spirit aura – the one that extends furthest from the body. In your own time, explore the edges of this aura and feel the difference in its vibration and resonance. When you are done, return to 2nd position and gradually bring your palms back together to 1st position, an inch apart and then *finally* allow them to touch.

This life-changing and simple exercise is designed to give you concrete proof that the presence of your soul's life force energy is real and not an abstract concept. You should now feel a strong sense of balance and inner peace. You have tuned yourself to the earth and the cosmos. Repeated use of this exercise will increase your psychic and spiritual awareness to ever finer degrees of consciousness and inspiration. The stronger you make your awareness of these fields, the better the worker you shall become.

With regard to the effect of touching your palms together at the end, this is to help restore any imbalance in the energy fields you may have inadvertently caused when accessing and manipulating them. It is also a way for you to close down without leaving your aura field open or disturbed in anyway. This is why it is important that when doing this exercise you are not interrupted. A disruption in the middle of something like this will leave you open to fatigue, stress and heightened sensitivity.

A further note on the spirit aura: Its shape is ovular and cuts off just below the knee and the top of the head. When spirits appear through this soul window they appear to float. The Chinese have a saying that dead people have no feet! We do have feet, of course, just not in this aura. This could be an explanation for 'floating phantoms'.

EXERCISE
Discerning the Auras and Energies of Another
For this you will need a sympathetic recipient, not someone who is in anyway negative to the practice. To apply the previous exercise to another person you should start by sitting them comfortably in a chair. You should stand behind with your hands at your side. You each take three relaxed, controlled breaths. After this, the sitter need do nothing more than sit quietly. Slowly lift your hands until they are either side of their head. Steadily move your hands away from the head until they are three feet apart, where the edge of the spirit aura is to be found. As before, gently bounce your hands to feel the strength of its influence. Now bring your hands up over the head without touching the crown and feel a shift in the magnetic field and temperature. You may find yourself experiencing a rocking sensation and that you might lose your balance, but this will not happen. It is a symptom of aura blending. Now bring your hands over the ears, all the time sensing and feeling the energy of the mental and emotional aura of the sitter.

Because you now know where these auras are situated, explore them with your hands and feel where they send you with their magnetic and fluid streams. Take your time doing this. Do not engage in wild hand movements or quivers.

To close, bring your hands back to where you started and then place them on the sitter's shoulders. This is a gentle way of letting them know you have finished and they can come around in the event they found themselves deep under the influence.

So how do you feel? Are you aware of the changes and heightened awareness of each aura? What about the colours you both may have perceived? It is not unusual for colours and spirit sensations to be perceptible throughout this exercise. With your sitter, discuss what you felt. Also what you saw, where and what form it took. Do not get caught up in trying to explain everything. Even for masters, the process and full interpretation is still not fully understood. This is a simple exercise – not a complex one.

As an alternative approach, why not try this exercise with lights dimmed and see if you can make out the aura fields and colours? A low watt red light is considered to be of the greatest benefit to seeing this way.

Chapter Six

Colours and Their Meanings

The Code of the Spirit; the Eyes of the Soul

If you are asked to think of a favourite colour, you can see it in your mind's eye. Sometimes the spirit will work with you this way if you are so constituted. Other times you may see colours as light on or to the side of people, animals and occasionally plants and flowers. These colours have meanings and although we can refer to a helpful colour guide contained in this part, experience tells us we build up our own personal colour interpretation. This then becomes our unique diagnostic tool.

When we perceive the aura we see within it colours in various shapes and forms. These colours are the code of the spirit: the eyes of the soul. In order to crack this code we need to attune ourselves and apply a degree of discipline to the process (*see* Meditation). It is important to note that there are both positive and negative connotations and denotations with colours. For instance, red can mean rage but it can also symbolise energy and vitality. There is already an existing system of colour interpretation universally accepted amongst practitioners and with experience and practice you will find it proudly coexisting alongside that which will be your own system colours. You should think of them as your colours, therefore your messages and your meanings should be derived from them. What red may mean to you can, and often does, mean something entirely different to someone else. All living energy is colour.

Can colours colour our moods?

Is it important where we see colour?

Is colour a form of communication?

The answer to these questions is yes! The Principles of Colour

Guide given here below is a straightforward diagnostic device. It can be referred to by student and teacher alike when colours seem difficult to interpret. Remember, if you can perceive a colour, you can interpret it. However, it is also nice to have an aid to follow which can widen your spiritual vocabulary if needed. So, when you find yourself inarticulate about a colour, see the colour part for inspiration and guidance, printed here in the order they appear in the spectrum ray with some overlapping and additional shades.

WHITE
POSITIVE ASPECT: Comprising all the colours of the spiritual light spectrum, chaste, pureness, oneness, defining, cleansing, insight, harmony, redeeming, heavenly.
NEGATIVE ASPECT: Bland, vague, hiding a truth, uncaring, stark, lost, soulless, discarded.

RED: PLANET MARS, RAY. Symbolises life.
Red is also a SUN colour and can represent vibrancy.
POSITIVE ASPECT: Life energy, strength, power, vitality, courage, desire, passions, determination, fight, strength of mind, vigour, warm and affectionate, leadership.
NEGATIVE ASPECT: Domineering, flatterer, vain, aggressive, bad tempered, rage, danger (especially when seen in conjunction with BLACK).

ORANGE: SPHERE – The SUN, RAY. Symbolises health.
Orange is also a SUN colour and can represent vibrancy.
POSITIVE ASPECT: Optimism, natural energy, intuitive, inner strength, warmth of personality, strong willed, stimulating, enthusiasm, confidence, courage, vitality, unselfishness, energetic, healing and sensitivity.
NEGATIVE ASPECT: Selfishness, rude, ruthlessness, ambition, danger (especially when seen in conjunction with BLACK).

YELLOW: SPHERE – The MOON, RAY. Symbolises wisdom. Yellow is also a SUN colour and can represent vibrancy.
POSITIVE ASPECT: Mentally quick witted, intellectual, knowledge, cleverness, honourable, positive, study of higher things, self-control, patience, happiness, joyfulness, preservation, a very spiritual colour.
NEGATIVE ASPECT: Jealous, suspicious, cowardly, unfaithful, greedy, danger (especially when seen in conjunction with BLACK).

GREEN: PLANET – VENUS, RAY. Symbolises balance and calm.
POSITIVE ASPECT: Nature's colour, growth, healers, stamina, practical, sympathetic, intellectual, service, creativity, artistic, energy, harmony, nursing.
NEGATIVE ASPECT: Envy, jealousy, deceit, treachery.

TURQUOISE: PLANET - EARTH RAY. Symbolises life.
POSITIVE ASPECT: Mediumship, cooling, purity through hard work, observer.
NEGATIVE ASPECT: Lazy, ineffectual, seeking praise, greed, obesity.

BLUE: PLANET – MERCURY, RAY. Symbolises inspiration.
POSITIVE ASPECT: Water of life, caring, truth, fairness in all things, farseeing, free spirits, direct, good speakers, compassionate, nursing, faith, hope, devotion, honesty, sincerity, meditation, spiritual.
NEGATIVE ASPECT: Worry, depression, moody, over-reaction.

INDIGO: SPHERE – ALPHA CENTAURI, RAY. Symbolises solicitude.
POSITIVE ASPECT: Prayer, religious faith – especially when coupled with gold, ability towards clairvoyance, intuition, solitude, music-lover, devotion, faith.

NEGATIVE ASPECT: Introvert, dreamer, unhappy.

VIOLET: PLANET – NEPTUNE, RAY. Symbolises spiritual power.
POSITIVE ASPECT: True colour of the etheric body on earth, poetry, dedicated, deeply sensitive, sterling character, service, humility, mediumistic, maturity, mystic.
NEGATIVE ASPECT: Lack of understanding, a sense of loneliness and isolation, emotionally extreme.

PINK: Love, RAY.
POSITIVE ASPECT: Devotion, emotion, good health, sensitive, soothing.
NEGATIVE ASPECT: Over inflated ego, adversarial, impertinence.

BROWN
POSITIVE ASPECT: Study, earthiness, stability, basic, good listeners, protective, study of life.
NEGATIVE ASPECT: Stuck in a rut, depression, disappointment, low self-esteem, immovable.

GREY
POSITIVE ASPECT: Staid, functional, strong work ethic.
NEGATIVE ASPECT: Misguided in adherence to duty, tiredness, lack of imagination, uncertainty, down-putting, 'dirty/sooty/grimy' auric field denoting criminal tendencies, unpleasant, stubborn.

SILVER
POSITIVE ASPECT: Truth, love, devotion – particularly of the highest order.
NEGATIVE ASPECT: Lies, grief, deception – especially at the hands of a love partner.

GOLD

POSITIVE ASPECT: True spiritual attainment usually seen only in the mental and emotion aura about the head and placed there like a crown by the spirit. Sits on top of the mental and emotional aura denoting connections to high energies. Extremely rare!

NEGATIVE ASPECT: Self satisfying, greed, gambling, false façade, shallow, impulsive, fickle, insatiable avarice, false glory and its pursuit, enemy.

BLACK

POSITIVE ASPECT: Deepness of thought, supreme dedication to something, seriousness.

NEGATIVE ASPECT: Lack of communication, unfathomable, danger (especially when seen in conjunction with any of the three Sun colours).

Individually, silver and gold are generally agreed to be the only colours that will harmonise with any other colour. When seen in conjunction with another colour, they are thought to boost the power of that colour manifold. Conversely, black, when seen in conjunction with any other colour is considered to amplify many times its negative traits.

Note also that black, when in conjunction with either red, orange or yellow, act as nature's universal warning signs. For example bees, snakes and other poisonous and potentially harmful creatures have adopted these colour combinations to caution potential predators. This is no coincidence. When seen in the aura, great care should be taken to heed their warnings. Have you noticed how international warning signs adopt the same colour systems?

It is said that in past times we were better able to see the spirit colours that accompanied everyday communication between human beings. As you progress you will reawaken this means within yourself; you will begin to see things previously missed by you. This can be emotionally painful as well as rewarding. You will see and sense things that may hurt you or deeply affect you to the point of not being able to rest at night. One remedy is to accept heightened sensitivity as a very real force in your life, but not one that you should allow to control you. It never goes away and you must learn to deal with it if you are to succeed!

Here are a few examples of how colours, psychically observed, have found their way into everyday speech. For instance, when someone is telling you a lie or not being truthful with you, you may see silver grey on their tongue – 'speaks with a silver tongue'. With someone recovering from an illness or in good health you may perceive a visible pink glow about them – 'in the pink'. Something that appears either by way of an apport (an object materialised through space and time) or physical phenomena, or has been divinely inspired with a touch of genius is said to have come 'out of the blue'. The 'blue' in this instance represents spirit and not to be confused with 'a bolt out of the blue'. Comprised of the best qualities of red and blue, *purple* over the wise heart is a sign of supreme devotion, love and quest, hence 'a purple heart'. Green appears in the eyes when jealousy is the dominant emotion. Where danger is afoot, a yellow streak or line can be seen down a spine symbolising preservation – not cowardice.

Chapter Seven

Creating and Channelling Spirit Art

Through and by the hand of...

When it comes to describing the work of these exponents it is actually a misnomer to refer to them as *Psychic Artists*. They are *'Spirit Artists'* or *'Spirit Imagers'*. What they are illustrating comes through and by the hand of the spirit. The psychic artist on the other hand will only describe images of earthly origin or the material plane. This is further explained in Chapter Thirteen. What is called psychic and what is called spirit is a special area of study and time should be taken to learn the differences.

One should always be sceptical of an illustration by an artist that almost perfectly represents an earthly photograph of the departed soul. Why dress and adopt in visage and figure expression an exact copy of how one would have looked when on the earth plane? Such artwork is not considered to be of spirit origin. An attempt will be made here to show the difference between what is considered *psychic* art and *spirit imaging*, for contained within the aura is unlimited mental imagery. These are the images of every place you have ever been, everyone you have ever seen and everything you have ever done. The aura, which is your database, also holds information about your previous generations too, and as you develop your spiritual and psychic awareness, this information will be revealed to you. This latter part is also looked at in Chapter Thirteen (sympathetic vibrations of thought).

Those more closely associated with you in life will have a greater prominence in your aura field. These are the emanations the psychic artist will be sensitive to. For example, a man brings to the class a photograph of his mother together with a psychic drawing of her – the two are almost identical. Surely the psychic artist has merely picked up on an image of how the man's mother would have looked when on the earth plane from his own aura? Apparently, *yes*. For the purposes of this exercise, we will take it the mother is to the other side of life. His mother's spirit may or may not have been present at the time of the drawing; this is irrelevant. Incidentally, she need not even be in the spirit world at the time of the image's making for this type of work to be produced.

The true spirit imager will present on paper a picture of the man's mother in a pose and figure expression quite unique to her and not a copy of something captured by a camera, thereby creating an almost photographic likeness. It will be a picture that communicates that she is alive here and now, albeit in the hereafter.

When looking at true spirit art, you will note that there are no shadows, yet the images often appear to have extension in three dimensions, an effect which is ordinarily very hard to achieve on the flat plane of the canvas. Unlike psychic art, these examples appear alive. They show perfectly that spirit images are not photographs – they are representations! They capture the essence and vitality of the individual, almost caricature – yet at the same time, better than that.

As the spirit artist develops they may become aware of more than one influence working through them. Often they are not so much bombarded with information and imagery as actual vibrations of thought and varied levels of consciousness. In other words, as the *instrument*, they are at the gentle control of spirit guides. They cannot defy this basic premise or principle of operation. If they do then they lose their inspiration, the spirit leaves them, they can work no more and must put down their tools.

Enormous trust has to build between the worker and the operator. The artist must be brave, especially when working with expensive canvas and oil. The spirit will often inspire them to make a dramatic or sweeping movement of the brush, which seems to defy all logic. In the end, what is produced can be really quite spectacular.

It can be rare for the artist to know exactly what they are going to illustrate when working this way and this is perhaps the best way forward for you to develop your psychic and spiritual artistic skills. Often an artist will look blankly at their chosen media and will be inspired or directed to pick up a particular colour and begin applying it. Often they will be oblivious to what they are about to create. They will often be just as curious as any third party spectator as to the eventual outcome. Strictly speaking, in spirit art there is no such thing as 'a mistake'. Many times artists will find that what they thought was a mistake has turned out to be an integral part of the finished illustration in shape, form and colour.

There is something instantly identifiable about a picture that has come from the spirit world. It has a special life, light and luminosity all its own.

EXERCISE

Open yourself up using the meditation or crystal exercise but with special attention drawn to an area just to the back of your head at the centre known as the occipital lobe. Imagine a highly focussed inspirational beam striking this power centre and energising this spot. With practice, and in time, you will be able to switch this on almost at will. However, for now, be satisfied that this organic focal point represents the clear vision and analysis of what you receive from spirit as well as it being the seat of the inspirational, creative and imaginative area of what we shall call the spirit counterpart to the organ of the brain. This is why we can experience difficulty believing that what we are receiving is from outside and not created by our imagination. In time, and with practice, you will be able to distinguish that which comes from within and that which comes from without. The importance of the acknowledgment and developing of this psychic area cannot be underestimated, for you will use it and call upon it many times in the giving of inspirational speech, philosophy and all the creative faculties you may possess and demonstrate in future. Remember to close this part down in reverse of how you opened up when you finish your session otherwise you may not be able to sleep.

Whatever media you choose, i.e. watercolour, crayon, pastels or oils, the principles are the same. You have before you a blank sheet and a range of colours. You may find that by using a small meditation or even a crystal tuning, you can stream the creative and inspirational influence to finer stages of vision and under-standing. Having opened up, as previously described, you are now ready to work.

Students often find it helpful to touch their brow chakra, a point at the centre of your forehead. As you begin to work in the following way, this psychic point will continue to feel as though it were freshly touched by you. While this feeling is upon you, look at the blank whiteness and the colourful pallet before you. Switch your gaze between the two a number of times. What do you see? What do you feel? Perhaps your hand is tingling or has a strange force or energy about it now you've opened up to this way of working, as so many of the ancients had before you. You are drawn to a particular colour – one that stands out above all the rest, even if ever so slightly. Why does it appear so conspicuous? How is it so noticeable? Go to that colour and hold it in your hand. Where is it to be applied and in what way? You are a medium, albeit for colour, and as with mediumship, it is the total giving over of oneself as the instrument. Be brave. Apply the colour and see what shapes and structures take form. Now you have taken the first step in applying the colour, what happens next? What are you now stimulated to do? If this exercise is working for you, and it may take practice, then you should be pulling out the next and the next colour. Feel the energy starting to work with you as you apply more and more colours to the point where you do not want to stop. You become almost an observer to what *you* are doing! Feel the liberation.

EXERCISE
Producing Spirit Portraits

It is amazing what faces can be produced when working in a free and inspired way. One method for producing work of this nature is to gaze at the paper and look for an eye or eyes to appear gently in the whiteness. If you begin with the eyes then you cannot go wrong. Hold on to that image as you trace around them and slowly bring them to life. The eyeball is common in shape and form with the only real variant being its colour. Once these are illustrated you begin to get a sense of the eyelid, then the orbit and then the eyebrow. Already a personality is forming before you. You may notice the line of a cheekbone or perhaps a chin line too. Trace this out as well. Eventually a face will appear, but do not be surprised if you find you have imaged a cat or dog, for animals dwell in the spirit realms too. This can be a very rewarding and exciting way to work. It will develop you to ever higher degrees of realisation.

As you paint or draw these discarnate friendly spirits who wish to come through and sit for you, you will begin to pick up their memory links, feelings, their occupation, where they lived and in what era, but none of this is an essential requirement. It is fascinating to watch their form almost materialise before you. And as you fill in their neck and shoulders, you become aware of what type of clothing they may have worn.

A true spirit picture produced this way always shows a face of peace and serenity, free from the cares and burdens of this world. You may find that this spirit has had a long association with you and may have even been your guide. Or they may belong to someone else known to you. In this instance, your psychic awareness will tell you this image is for a certain other. If you do not already know, your spirit operator will help you find who it is. When placed correctly with the right seeking person, the joy felt on their part at this new image of their long lost loved one can be very rewarding for all concerned. And remember, when you are working for the higher good, your intuition becomes boosted immensely. You do not need to be a Leonardo. Some students produce wonderful caricature work this way, too, still carrying a unique likeness of the departed soul.

Chapter Eight

Producing Auragraphs for Yourself and Others

Maps of the Soul

Look at the aura as you would a flower. By reading its colours and condition it is possible to tell a lot about it. Is there is new growth, does it need more light, is it past its best, does it need more water, and so on. Reading the colours and energies of the aura is exactly the same. Just think for a moment how complex the human body is. The aura is infinitely more subtle and multi-faceted! When seen in its full glory, it is beyond all imagination and expectation. Unfortunately, when we read the aura we see only a small aspect of the greater whole. Students often think the aura is made up of primary colours or strange shaped psyche-delic splodges, but this is simply not so. Neither is it true that we go about in the spirit world with auras flashing or ablaze. The aura is seen only at the will and discretion of the individual concerned. And this leads us onto a very special point. Beyond being impinged upon to see an aura by the spirits, or your own natural psychic awareness reasons, you must never create an auragraph, an aura reading or discern another's aura without their permission. It is invasion of privacy, an unacceptable practice and an abuse of the ability! Without their consent, you may also draw the wrong conclusions. Further, the spirit intelli-gence will do no work of quality with you in the long run.

EXERCISE
Creating an auragraph. Duration, 20 – 30 minutes
Materials: white paper or canvas. Colour pencils, crayons, water colours, poster paints/acrylics or oils.

Method: Draw a circle to fit the page.

You may use this exercise to create an auragraph for yourself with a view to it being read by another. Or you can create one that can be read by you for another. Either way, meditate on your subject. This can include looking directly at them and then to your pallet of colours. Take three relaxed, controlled breaths. See to which you are more strongly drawn and then apply the colour to where you feel the push. You may find yourself shading-in colours or drawing little pictures or writing little words and names. Turn the whole thing upside down if necessary. You should also feel the spirit energy working through you; helping you to achieve a satisfactory and coherent outcome. Be aware also of subtle changes in vibration and in visual perception. For instance, you may see an outline of something before you, a shape or face. Ask your spirit friends to help you bring these things to life before you. Often a persistence in energy is experienced that makes it difficult for the student to stop.

There is no logical system in place for producing auragraphs, but some awareness teachers may suggest a timeline for the exercise such as the centre of the circle could represent the past, the middle perimeter could be where they are now, and anything produced outside of the circle could be related to the future such as specific events or aspirations.

When you feel you can do no more, finish by taking three relaxed and controlled breaths. Study the images. Sometimes holding it afar can make it possible to discern a holistic picture from the montage. At first, what you have produced may make no sense to you until you start explaining to the recipient why you chose the colours you did. Explain to them what you felt and do not be afraid to ask questions of them. You may also find that they can see things in the auragraph not immediately obvious to you. You can always refer to Chapter Six if you are stuck for an interpretation of a colour. It is a great way to work and to open your spirit and psychic faculties and invaluable in developing your clairvoyance. The auragraph is merely a physical representation of what the psychic eye sees and although working this way is essentially a psychic exercise, the spirits can easily find their way into the work produced.

Always be mindful too that you may be digging up the past when working this way. That is why a properly constituted student will endeavour to work with only the highest and the best at all times. Some students find their forte producing this work and go on to realise ever more detailed and intricate work, including glimpses of the life beyond. No matter what level you are at, auragraph creation can be very rewarding overall, not least because a tangible artefact has been produced that can become a cherished possession over time and read over again by different mediums.

Chapter Nine

The Art of Scrying and How to Do It

Looking Beyond the Senses

Scrying is an ancient practice often described as the ability to interpret shape and form in materials such as water, smoke, crystals, clouds or even the folds of a cloth. Practitioners generally favour materials that have properties of luminescence, translucence or reflection. But scrying can be exercised with almost anything random or fractal. Tarot readers will often scry into their cards for messages, even though they may not always be aware of it. To the worker in the field, these chance patterns *can* be used to communicate messages and meanings to ourselves and through ourselves to others. It is true we can discern faces in clouds and trees almost at will but, strange as it may seem, the physical eye sees nothing. What we perceive is created by the brain. The eye is merely a camera with automatic focus, exposure and white balance settings. 'Seeing', on the other hand, is a high-order brain function. The detection and identification of patterns is something learned from childhood. As a student, you are like a child again, learning to read this new world of spiritual and psychic awareness that has been reopened to you.

At first nothing may seem to make sense. However, as you learn more about these other worlds (hidden from our usual gaze by the thinnest of veils) and begin to open the doors to perception, an interpretation of what you are drawn to slowly begins to emerge. Simply put, the spirit uses patterns to communicate messages to you and may ask you to relay them to others if, when and where required. What you are accessing and utilising is the creative and inspirational facet of the brain.

So let us say that within a crystal ball you are drawn to see (what looks to you like) a dragon. There is *no* dragon within the ball. It is purely your ability to decode the shape and form of a dragon within it under an inspired stimulus. People will say, *'Oh this is just my imagination'*. Knowing the difference forms an important mechanism of psychic science. Only when you master it through practice and experience will you be able to distinguish that which you are creating within you and what you are receiving from outside of you. This is an important key to looking *beyond* the five senses.

As a human being, you are able to imagine and build models of the world in your mind and thereby guess the probable outcomes of events already set in motion. The spirits use this ability within you. From their communication you interpret and express what you are being told.

In seeing images you will also *feel* what they mean. You should not forget that when you are practicing the discipline, everything is a communication! Even your failure to communicate should itself be taken as a form of communication. Your perception of a block can carry meaning to the recipient or give indication as to their current disposition. And although others will often be able to see what you see, do not expect all to distinguish the same as you, for each person decodes in their own unique way.

While we should reach further than our grasp, do not be down hearted or disappointed by not being able to achieve a desired level of attainment. You must be greedy and use everything they send you to work with, however subtle or delicate. You will never get all the answers but that should not preclude you from asking, 'who, what, why, when, where and how'!

Before attempting the more traditional materials such as water, stone, crystal, fire, smoke, you may like to try paints. This can be very rewarding and will train your psychic eye to be more discerning. The principles are the same.

EXERCISE
Scrying With Paint Patterns
Materials needed:
1 sheet of A4 white card.
Three poster paints or oils of red, blue and yellow and an additional colour of warm cream or magnolia to create the very best results.

Method:

1. Decide if this work you are creating is for you or someone else. If it is your first time then yourself first would be the natural order.
2. Although you may not think so, all workers operate in an altered state or light trance. Tune in and open up in your own unique way.
3. Place the card flat on a table.
4. See in what order the colours are to be used.
5. Under 'guidance', take one at a time, in roughly equal measure and squeeze onto the card from a height of approximately two feet. Apply in an almost random way
6. With care, fold the card over and pressing gently down, push out from the fold to the edges of the sheet to allow for good coverage
7. Slowly peel open to reveal pattern and allow to dry

How to Read It

This is one of the better scrying exercises because it requires some work to put it together and the images produced can be quite detailed and realistic. Share the finished work and see what others can read into it too. If scrying works for you and you are able to see worlds within worlds, move onto other media. However, it is also worth noting that reading with the traditional materials that scryers use can be very difficult – especially for the novice who may discern only one or two things from their chosen media but not enough to give a good and accurate message or full reading.

Chapter Ten

How to Produce Teachings and Philosophy Through Inspirational Writing and Speech

Operating the Perfect Channel

Philosophy gives substance to what we believe and teach in the psychic and spiritual awareness workshop. In general, we can take philosophy to mean the study of

- Life
- Knowledge
- Being
- Thought
- God

We shall take a theory or set of ideas based around one or more of these themes as the inspiration for the writing part of our exercise. You may adapt the template at a later stage to suit.

Inspiration is the creative stimulus or influence filling both heart and soul with enthusiasm. When you, as the channel, are inspired to give philosophy, the spirit operates the perfect channel.

EXERCISE
Writing Spirit Inspired Philosophy
Open up as described in Chapter Three but with special focus on the crown and the brow chakras. You may want to momentarily physically touch these points. Also, send special energy to your hand – one of the main receptors in the body and spirit body for information. Now pick one or more of the following about which to write.

- Love
- Time
- Fear
- Healing
- Death
- Beauty
- Spirituality
- Wisdom
- Hatred
- Higher and lower self

Even with the help of those in spirit, it can still be one per cent inspiration and ninety-nine per cent perspiration. Your initial writings may at first be self-centric, but in time these will give way to more externally inspired words. This is not to be confused with automatic writing – a completely different phenomena. Once you begin the writing process, whether by pen or PC, you may find it hard to stop. Spiritual places, dimensions and concepts can flood your mind, rewarding you and pushing you on to ever deeper expressions. A light overshadowing (slight trance or altered state) within your aura together with an energy field forming around your writing or typing hands is a common occurrence. Norma Meagher's example in the meditation chapter is a good illustration of what can be achieved and, as she did too, feel free to share your writings. We learn together in partnership as 'sensitives' (through these inspired teachings) not only to reinforce the old ways, but also bring about new ways of exploring communication and understanding between us and the higher side of life.

There is a type of writing called Stream of Consciousness, which you might like to try and can begin quite simply by drawing a doodle on the page such as a sacred symbol or maybe a rose. It works better if the writing appears on the same page as the image because the energies blend better this way. Alternatively, form something similar in your head and begin writing about what it means to you.

Speaking Inspired Philosophy

Some students may find the speaking part of this exercise easier than writing. If that is the case you should record what is said with a view to playback. The only difference in opening up is that you would not energise the hand but the throat chakra. Also include a gentle physical touch to that area. As with the writing component, what we are looking to achieve here is a degree of teaching from the spirit realms that goes beyond our conscious volition, free from the constraints of ego and convention. Silly booming voices should be avoided and are an instant indicator of ego and fakery. This type of work is not the preserve of masters but open to us all to explore the inner workings of the mind and soul and its relationship to that which we see and that which created us.

Automatic Writing

This is indeed a very rare and exceptional talent which, like so many of the spiritual gifts, is historically littered with fraud and misunderstanding. However, we shall not concern ourselves with anything other than its method and outcome. In theory, the talent can be demonstrated in a blacked out room with only a pen and paper before the channel. It is often demonstrated under deep trance with the instrument completely unaware of what they are writing. A distinctive hand style from that of the channel will clearly be discernable. Even favouring the other hand is not unusual. The student may begin by allowing the spirit operators to manipulate the hand randomly, producing erratic scribbles and the like, which eventually develop into legible text.

Chapter Eleven

Psychometry:
What is It and How is It Done?

Psychometry is part of psychic phenomena and is a type of extra-sensory perception. It is sometimes taken to mean the measure of the soul. The term was coined by Joseph Rhodes Buchanan in 1842, six years before the Fox sisters began the misnomer that is so called Modern Spiritualism. He described what he called 'The mental telescope', saying, 'The past is entombed in the present' (Manual of Psychometry: The Dawn of a New Civilisation, 1893). It has also been known as psychoscopy and although official acknowledgement is scarce, it has been widely reported as being used by members of the law enforcement communities in cold case files, albeit as a last resort. The practice relies solely on the psychic medium handling an artefact to acquire hitherto unknown information about events in the object's history as well as the nature of its owner(s).

Some very important points to remember are that physical, inorganic objects of the material plane do not possess a spirit or enable the future to be told and neither are they a means by which spirit communication can be conducted. But the practice of psychometry *can* open the door to the spirit and aid the process. However, they can be a store for psychic energy and so too can animate and organic objects such as people, animals, flowers and water – things we shall come onto for our practical workshop exercise.

Psychometry is the ability to read the emanations left on objects through time. It is also the capacity to ascertain infor-mation about a person or experience by handling items connected with them. To keep it simple, consider there are just two parts of an object's history impressed upon the medium.

These are as follows:

A time when the object came into being.
Its history thereafter.

Before developing the student's skill with personal items belonging to others, the group would do well to start out with water, sand, flowers and photographs. These have become amongst the most common and successful materials used to practice psychometry.

Sand, because of its crystalline formation and properties.
Water, for its super complex fluidity and hidden properties.
Flowers, not only for their beauty, but as a natural living thing.
Photographs, not only as an explicit representation or likeness of a dear departed one, but also for the saturation of love embossed upon the paper by the one left behind.

Because psychometry deals with the life of the recipient almost directly through the mental telescope, be aware that sometimes these sessions can become quite emotionally draining if not checked or reined in. Care, as always, should be taken with what is given out at such assembly. Hence the need for an experienced, compassionate leader. It is considered prudent to request that items placed upon the table are bereft of emotional scars unless healed by love.

Psychometry Technique

Hold the object and view it through the psychic third eye brow chakra. Some people feel that holding it to this point improves accuracy. What are the first impressions?

- Are they emotional?
- Are they visual?

- Are they physical?
- Are they a mixture of things?
- How did the recipient acquire it?
- Was it a gift and if so, from whom?
- Did they find it and if so, where and in what circumstance?
- Or did they buy it?

After a time, there will be no need to engage in this type of internal dialogue as experience will give rise to information that will come flooding through.

EXERCISE

The following can be completed with or without the fledgling having knowledge of the sitter already. Though it is worth noting, the reliability and quality of the reading may suffer where the fledgling has a degree of familiarity with a prospective sitter. If working in a regular group then familiarity can breed easy, uncomplicated, undemanding messages – so be aware. Often the best results are achieved where stranger reads for stranger.

Open up with an active or guided meditation for psychometry (Chapter Three). This may involve activating certain psychic centres of the body or attuning oneself to the harmonies and frequencies of the group members. Special attention should be made to the base chakra (the power), the third eye (seeing), the finger tips (the receptors) and the throat or voice chakra for articulation of the message.

Sand Readings

Place a quantity of sand in a mid-sized bowl. Where possible, fresh beach sand should be used. Without the knowledge of the novice, ask a sitter to place their hand in the bowl for a few moments leaving a perceptible handprint. Invite the reader to place their hand in the imprint and give a reading. After the opening remarks have been made, the recipient should be revealed to the reader and enquiry made of their accuracy. If the student feels sufficiently confident, they may like to continue on with the reading. The sand being used should be read the same way as if holding an object for psychometry. Do not worry about contamination when the sand is passed around the group. Resettling it with several shakes and starting afresh has the effect of virtually neutralising the previous impression.

Water Readings

Fill a bowl with a quantity of lukewarm water. Invite or choose a sitter to place their hand in the water for a few moments. Reading the water is an adaptation of the sand exercise. If convenient, fresh water can be used each time.

Flower Readings

Described as earth's precious gems, flowers are a great way to begin one's psychic awareness reading. Unlike the previous two examples, flowers are living things and like photographs, have a scrying element to their interpretation. Ask the group to each bring to the class a flower cut from a garden that should have been handled by them exclusively. Set out a table large enough to ensure that each flower can be isolated in its own space without fear of contamination from another. Ask the students to attached a number or raffle ticket to the flower with them retaining the duplicate. In the event of it being a large class, this simple provision eliminates the possibility of confusion over choosing flowers of the same variety; for instance, where three people have each brought a yellow freesia.

Perhaps the beginning of the stalk could be taken to be the beginning of the recipient's life. And as the student rises up through the flower, a story, together with their thoughts and aspirations, may begin to emerge out of the bloom. The scrying part can be something as simple as damage to a petal, the appearance of fragility in a branch, a new bud, or the feeling of influence and control derived from the stem's flexibility and strength. These are the types of things the reader should consider.

Objects Placed on a Table

Related closely to the flower exercise, ask this time that they bring something with a history to place on the workshop table. Then ask the student to choose an object from the table they are particularly drawn to. Proceed as outlined in the above part, Psychometry Technique.

Photographs

As a rule, ask that only one person be in the frame and further, that they are now in spirit. The emotional aspect of this activity cannot be underestimated. Even approaching the table with so many images on, including children, animals, family and friends, can be quite overpowering and yet very beautiful to experience. Trust in spirit guides, friends and helpers will come into its own at a time like this. Photographs, particularly cherished ones, hold tremendous power for their owners. In the scrying part of this exercise, it may be possible to see the face change. Where spirit are present, their manipulation can mean a slight transformation in how the image is decoded by the brain. When this happens, the reader may notice a shift in consciousness and a change in vibration. A spirit link could be said to now be established. The reading may switch at this point to clairvoyance.

These exercises aid the sensitivity of the fledgling in tuning to psychic frequencies. After a time and with practice, they may become aware of different levels of consciousness working through them, in difference to those that come from within them. In time, confidence can grow to the point of not requiring 'props' to read. However, even the most experienced exponents still enjoy simple psychometry and the wonderful benefits it can bring.

Chapter Twelve

The Circle and How to Run One

Some personal hints on an approach to the discipline, though not in any particular order.

Circles fall into a number of categories. There is the home circle and the circle of the awareness centre or church. The home circle is usually constituted of people who are friends and wish to explore and experiment free from the conventions of an organisation. At what we shall call church level, there are three types of circle. These are the Open Circle, the Advanced Circle and the Development Circle – their names may differ from place to place.

1. Pick a convenient day in the week upon which to meet in a suitable, quiet location free from outside interferences. Never be late! Always arrive in good time. Send your thoughts out through the day of nice, spiritual things.

2. Preparing the room. Make sure it is free of odours. No smoking allowed in the room at anytime during the interim periods. Keep it dust free. Remember, *you* control the light in the room. Make sure, if desirable and for certain types of mediumship, that full blackout is achievable. The temperature of the room should be comfortable – a thermometer would be handy. Seating should be of reasonable quality. The general rule all round should be – the less physical distractions, the better.

3. The sitters should have preferably showered on the day of sitting. They should refrain from wearing perfumes or aftershaves. Bright clothing, glistening jewellery, and so

forth, are to be avoided. Big meals are not a good idea before sitting as up to three quarters of our body's energy will be taken up by the human digestive system. This causes drowsiness and will make it hard for the sitter to maintain full devotion. No alcohol whatsoever to be consumed on the day of sitting!

4. You must strongly question your reasons for sitting. Circles should not last longer than one hour. All sitters should be in a healthy state of mind, body and spirit.

5. A good, strong and loving circle leader is required – a medium that can tune-in and know what is going on and where everyone is at and which gift is to be developed and in whom. They must command the respect of all.

6. Each person should know exactly why he or she is sitting in the circle. People should know who their doorkeeper is. Each person should be able to sit properly and not fidget. Though not essential, they should sit in the same space each time.

7. Do not be disappointed if a circle doesn't feel right. It is simply an indication that you need to keep looking. The right *blend* is essential. It takes a special generosity of spirit to firstly sit and secondly sit for others. The uncontrolled ego and any form of self is enemy to the progress of the circle. Little, if any, work will take place in a circle that is not welcoming to our spirit friends and spirit power.

8. Considered 'old fashioned', the singing or playing of a loved one's favourite song may still be a desired way of making contact. And if sung by the group, it can lift the atmosphere, raise the vibrations and get the energies

going. Is your circle welcoming to our spirit friends? A good tester question might be, *'If you were in the spirit world now, would you give up your time to come here tonight?'*

9. Chakras, if they work for you, may be a desirable way of opening up the channels. Be very careful where these sacred centres are concerned. If you have not mastered them then do not use them. These sacred organs will open up automatically if you are working correctly and will duly close when you are finished. It is essential that each sitter knows how to close themselves down (Chapter Three).

10. Remember, never blame the spirit world for what you may feel is a failure or even the fault of yourselves – spirit knows best! They can only be as good as the material they have been given to work with. The better the discipline of the circle, then so better shall the results be. And remember to enjoy your sitting!

Running an Open Circle

Try to get the composition of the circle right from the outset. This means having,

- a leader
- a medium
- a circle recorder
- a novice
- and sitters.

The beauty of the open circle is that its format can be altered to suit. Almost unique to tips and hints number 5 in this section, the open circle leader need not be a clairvoyant but should endeavour to have the services of a good medium in attendance.

The leader should be able to monitor, direct and analyse proceedings along the right lines and be regarded as being in supreme control. The circle members should also discipline themselves along these lines and follow the instructions of the leader almost without question, unless this goes against an individual's principles or moral code. That said, it should also be remembered that much of this work is experimental.

EXERCISE

Start the circle in a relaxed way with controlled deep breaths followed by an opening prayer or reading from a book or something penned through and by the hand of a sitter (something they might like to share). In the case of a prayer or incantation, this can be a delegated task given to one whom will benefit most from the responsibility. The leader may then want to entrust a simple opening up technique to another member or, alternatively, conduct it themselves. There are plenty of these procedures available, but for the purposes of this type of gathering, the rule is to keep it simple. The open circle is free from the stricter disciplines of the closed circle.

The circle leader will intuitively know what is going on in the circle at all times and will nip in the bud any theatrics to do with faux trance and other such 'taking over'. Trance in particular is not part of the open circle. As its name implies, the circle is open to all: newcomer and regular alike. Trance can alarm the newbie and the reasons for its exclusion really should be self-evident.

The medium is the circle's link with the spirit. If you have more than one medium present then the circle leader will only give the floor to one speaker at a time. The medium and all contributors should stand to speak and sit when finished. This informs all parties who has the floor and when they are finished. Another reason for the one-at-a-time rule, particularly where novice mediums are concerned, is the leader and principle medium must hear what is being said and, where applicable, reign in a rogue messenger or ambiguous or flawed communication. Sitting in circle can cause people to behave strangely and give out what we shall call 'questionable' things, so a gentle but firm hand is sometimes needed. The spirit never cause fright or harm anyone, so let that be your guide in determining whether a word is needed or not.

Strange as it may seem, mediums do not always make the best circle leaders as they can be prone to the temperamental sensitivity, vibrations and moods of the gathering. The more experienced medium and leader might like to bring one or more novices to the open circle in order to demonstrate their clairvoyance in a friendly environment, more conducive and better suited to their beginner status.

Students of the awareness class should also be encouraged to bring their talents to the open circle, which is considered the demonstration forum for the forward looking awareness class. For instance, those who compose poetry, spirit writings, aura graphs, philosophy and so on, should be encouraged to share them here. Awareness classes can stagnate from time to time so fresh faces and environments will reinvigorate the work the students are doing. The circle leader will explain this to newcomers at the circle.

Healing is not a good idea in the open circle because its vibrations are slow, whereas clairvoyance is fast. It is often a good idea to record the circle either electronically or by taking notes. Much valuable information has been lost through failing to document information received from the higher side.

Depending on the size of the group, the circle leader will call time with the following in mind. They will go around the circle, giving a brief minute or two to each person and ask them what they got from the circle. Many times people will say they received little or nothing, but once they begin talking, the circle leader may have difficulty getting them to stop. The leader will also be a clock-watcher, keeping proceedings to within the hour.

This makes people hungry to come to the next meeting and they will be willing to better focus themselves next time around because they will now know there is a duration limit in place. Open-ended circles eventually fail or are seldom as well attended in the long run. The leader will then delegate the closing down of the group to an appropriate person, which may turnout to be themselves where none other is forthcoming.

Chapter Thirteen

What is 'Psychic'?

Superior sensitivity to mental and physical processes

There is literally a world of difference between the psychic medium and the spirit medium. Many people are not aware of this and quite often confuse (for example) the tarot reader with the spiritual medium. While natural mediums are few and far between, psychics by comparison are abundant. A medium has to be a psychic but a psychic need not be a medium. Everyone is psychic to a greater or lesser extent. Only by developing your psychic ability will you become a better instrument. Take Jesus and Moses for example. They were only able to manifest the spirit and prophesise because of their astonishing psychic capability. The psychic will generally only pick up earthly conditions in respect of a living person, place or object. They are not linking to the spirit world, though they can do without realising it (for spirits will use whatever channel is available to them). Psychics are sensitive to emanations in the aura fields, latent energies and impressions left on inanimate objects and places. This is because whatever we do, wherever we go, we leave impressions. The psychic has a heightened sensitivity to these energies present within a place or emitted from a person. Their sensitivity will manifest through one or more of their fives senses, i.e. they may hear, see, feel, smell or taste – including combinations of these.

To explain in greater depth we need to create a hypothetical reading with a psychic. How many times have you heard it said that a certain psychic was able to tell someone all about themselves? The psychic related to our recipient the following:

(a) They suffered a terrible illness when they were at school.

(b) The psychic suggested they 'go for' a business idea.

(c) A rickety old staircase they were concerned about in their house was mentioned and they were warned to 'be careful'.

(d) They were even told how much money they had in their pocket.

(e) The psychic then went on to describe their deceased mother, perfectly.

Amazing perhaps, but not where psychic science is concerned. These examples are quite common in the regular awareness class of any forward-looking centre where the students are encouraged to develop their psychic ability. *The stronger the psychic, the better the medium!* It is not important for the psychic to know the science they are using anymore than a car driver needs to be a mechanic. So, using the mechanics of this science, let us look again what is actually going on?

The aura is an invisible field of energy that surrounds all living things. It is the energy of the spirit and in turn, the spirit is the eternal part of any living thing. The energies and fields of the aura are created by the divine spark situated within the mental and emotional nimbus of the head. Your aura is a database containing information on everything to do with you; every thought you have ever had, every action you have ever made and every deed you have ever done in your life. It also contains your complete medical history as well as all your hopes, wishes, dreams and fears.

It could be argued that the client knew how much they had in their purse already. This may have been prominent in their mind at that particular time and the psychic has merely picked up on this. Remember, so often people say that they were *'told all about themselves'*.

Where the illness in youth is alluded to, depending on the

nature of the infirmity, this is usually read from the physical aura, though if it affected their mental state it would be quite possible to read the condition from there too. All the auras give good indication as to past and present disorders.

The staircase they were warned about would have been prominent in the mental and emotional aura too. Our client's worry over this represents a fear and concern, which the psychic has picked up on. In reality, the fear may be, and often is, a reality solely in the mind of the client. It does not mean they are going to come to grief on the staircase.

Regarding the business idea, this is represented as a dream and, in essence, may only ever be that and nothing more. Our client is the perhaps the kind of person who is a dreamer by nature and has a history of follies. Her dream may be to set up a shop in another part of the country in which she sees herself becoming a success. The psychic picks up on this and reads it back as a message to her that she must sell-up, move location and start a business. Astounded the psychic has told her this, she concludes without question that it must be true. Her poverty of knowledge concerning how psychic science works is, most likely, going to leave her high and dry. This is where personal responsibility on the part of the student of psychic science needs to be strictly exercised. An unscrupulous or ego driven psychic may exploit a vulnerable recipient this way.

The student must be careful with the information they give off when learning and applying the lessons of working on a purely psychic vibration without the spiritual constituent part well and truly in place! You are the control and you are accountable for everything you say. This is not an attack on psychics – just those without personal responsibility.

Where the recipient's mother is concerned, the psychic has read an earthly picture of her from the client's auric field – in this instance, the mental and emotional aura. The mother may or may not be present at the time of the reading. This is irrelevant. The psychic merely reads a picture of what this lady looked like when she was on the earth plane together with her illnesses, style of clothes and so on. To further illustrate this, our client has a liking for, say, John Lennon. The psychic sees a mental picture of John Lennon with our client and states, 'I see John Lennon with you. I can see him clearly in my mind.' It does not mean that John Lennon is actually present.

The aura also contains much about the past generations of our families. This is a special area of study called 'sympathetic vibrations of thought'. These are very special indeed. When our client walked into the room, she brought with her all her history, everyone she had ever met and everything she had ever done. This is also how the psychic reader can allude to something that was not part of the client's thinking, and indeed perhaps had not been so for some time.

So how do they predict the future? How is that possible?

If we look anecdotally at stories of prediction, *strictly* in the psychic sense, they are most often the probable outcome of events already set in motion. For example, the rickety staircase at home represents a fear. On a sympathetic vibration of thought, the psychic has become aware of this and interprets the vision by telling our recipient they see an accident to do with this. Sure enough, this is what eventually happens. But because we are talking here purely on a psychic level, this message would be considered as the probable outcome of an event already set in motion.

What about disasters such as those reported in the news? How come people often accurately predict these events before they happen? Again, applying the precognitive laws of psychic science we clearly see that these cataclysmic events represent a probable outcome set in motion, whether it is shanties built on areas prone to landslides or peoples forced to live on flood plains.

Concerning future events, the laws governing time, as with space, are still not fully understood. So we must view things with a clear and open mind. Our understanding of these things will most likely change hence from what they are at present. Future time can be previewed as a vision graphically played out in the mind of someone attuned to such time and space anomalies. These are not read from the aura but from what is sometimes called the akasha or ether.

So to summarise, the psychic is someone blessed with an inborn sensitivity of varying degrees to the emanations present within places or given off by individuals. They possess extrasensory perception particularly in areas such as healing and clairvoyance. We have yet to achieve a consummate understanding of psychic science and without development in the novice it cannot be easily controlled. It can also be misdiagnosed as a mental illness, which is why from the start we are required to be strong in mind, body and spirit. It should also be noted that psychics can link in with discarnate spirits but often they simply read the auras of individuals and the latent atmospheres and vibrations of places. By linking to the aura of a person, the psychic exponent will often give readings based on the past and present conditions of the sitter to do with relationships, health, material considerations, emotional states and future concerns.

Chapter Fourteen

Developing and Practicing Mediumship

The total giving over of oneself as the instrument

The term mediumship is used here because clairvoyance implies a raw ability without development, whereas the former, as with craftsmanship, implies discipline, control and mastery of a natural talent. All mediums are psychic – not all psychics are mediums.

So What is a Medium?

A medium is a go between, a messenger, if you like. They have developed their psychic sensitivities to the point where they can sense the presence of spirits, receive and accurately interpret messages from them and relay them on to recipients. In addition to being psychically aware, they are also sensitive to the energy fields and emanations that come from the spirit world and surround all living things. The true medium will have what the ancients called *nous*. They will know the spirit world do not interfere in your life and that your decisions are your own. Over their earth years and through the evolution of their soul, the medium will have build up an invaluable wealth of experience. They will be able to offer help and advice with authority and will openly admit to that of which they have little knowledge or experience.

Ego and Apostasy

A true spiritual medium will recognise in themselves the higher and lower self. When we as human beings act in a negative way or allow negative thoughts to dominate our spiritual self then we are using the lower side of our nature. When we are loving, giving and generous, we are using the higher self. The spiritual medium will endeavour always to operate within the higher self half.

They will also have gone through a significant number of dreadful and at the same time liberating experiences including one known as the disintegration of the ego. This will include a steady loss over time of some family and friends at the expense of gaining new ones more accepting of their chosen path. They will question the entire *who, what, why, when, where* and *how* of their existence and that which surrounds them. These questions, and many others, will assume a greater significance in the true spiritual medium's life at the risk of mentally destroying them. This path, especially for some, will expose every weakness and flaw they have. This abandonment of which we speak is a natural progression and we should not confuse the process with that offered by branded, corporatized religions, which when psychologically profiled reveal an entity determined to destroy families, relationships and free thinking! The very best mediums abandon previously held religious beliefs in favour of *spiritual* ones and make a true connection to the pleroma without intercessors and liturgy. Hence, true mediums will not describe themselves as religious people, but spiritual ones, albeit with failings.

There is nothing wrong with ego – we all have one. Without it we would never leave the house. It is when the negative ego is out of control or gains the upper hand that problems occur. So, there is the good ego and the bad ego. People have long debated when the ego begins. Some have suggested that when a child looks in the mirror and for the first time recognises the reflection as their own, the ego begins.

What is Spirit?

Spirit could be defined as the eternal part of any living thing. To be truly called a spiritual medium, one should have a further quality – that of spirituality. And the quality of the mediumship produced should be directly proportional to this. The medium will have possibly sat for many years (though this is not always necessary) and will have gone through many tests, some heart-breaking and soul destroying, to achieve a standard of development that is consistent with being a worthy vessel, instrument and ambassador for the other side. This life struggle forms an integral part of their groundwork.

Guides

Working with the mediums are spirit guides and helpers. A spirit guide, or guardian angel, will have been with the medium from *before* the day they were born to an earthly life and will most likely have lived through numerous incarnations with them. Guides are not relatives or friends; they are highly developed spirits who see only the best in the medium. Guides can do very little unless empowered and invoked by the medium. Through a hierarchy of knowledge, they can see further ahead and thereby inspire the medium with prophecy, foresight and precognition. These guides, in turn, work for those above them, and so on it goes all the way to the pleroma.

They are also known as spirit operators. Mediums cannot insist on anything from spirit guides. The relationship between medium and guide is not reliant on the medium acquiring detailed knowledge of their guide in order to work with them. Spirit guides often only reveal themselves over time. It is not unusual for a medium to have received only several communications from their guide across a generation of years. Like the medium on the earth plane, they too have to learn the mechanics, laws, codes and language of spirit communication from their side also. They have chosen to carry out this work in order to aid humanity, and for the people of earth to better understand their true nature and reason for being.

Helpers

These spirits have a particular developed quality they bring to the medium for a specific time. These qualities can run along the lines of occupation or trait. They may have skills in music, diplomacy or have a shared similar experience to something the medium is going through or dealing with at this time. They blend with the medium for a time consistent with learning a new skill or dealing with a new situation. Helpers are like the volunteers of the spirit world. They are not usually family or friend (though in certain cases are) and for the most part may not have been known to the medium in this or any previous life. They are human beings who have lived an earthly life and will work with many others on the earth plane too. A guide however, will work exclusively with the medium.

What the Medium Does

Although the 'medium' is a 'clairvoyant' and acts as a 'channel', there is a difference between all three expressions and we should endeavour to avoid confusion. The term 'channel' can be applied to the medium and the clairvoyant. But it is important to note that channelling can be learned, whereas clairvoyance and mediumship are abilities inherent from birth. The difference between these latter two are already discussed in the opening paragraph.

We can ask no more of the spirit than to prove (through the medium) they are there and nothing else. The spiritual medium will practice what they preach and will refuse no one, in genuine need, a service. This could be why many are called, but so few are chosen! The medium blends or attunes with the sitter. By doing this they open a channel to the spirit. The type of channel depends on the medium's type of gift. These are through, as well as over and above the five senses we possess and can be any one or combination of the following:

- Clairvoyance is to clearly see spirit.
- Claircognizance (term rarely used) is to clearly know or have an inherent understanding of spirit.
- Clairaudience is to clearly hear spirit.
- Clairsentience is to be clearly aware of spirit. This can include touch, smell and taste.

Using a particular faculty, the medium observes and passes on information to the sitter. Sometimes, when later asked to recall particulars, they may occasionally experience a slight difficulty because they work in an altered state of consciousness or light overshadowing under spirit operators.

Considered a good basis for communication technique, 'Spiritualist' mediums endeavour, as best they can, to work on the *Contact, Evidence, Reason for coming* and *Tidy-up* (C.E.R.T.) principle delineated thus:

Contact
They will establish a strong link with a particular person in the spirit. The medium will be able to keep hold of this contact and offer proof or evidence that they are whom they say. The medium will be able to tell the sitter who their contact is. This can be done either by name, connection to them, or both.

Evidence
By evidence we mean finding, with a recognised degree of certainty, the identity of the spirit involved. This is not neces-sarily the type of evidence that would stand up in a court of law – 'offer' being the operative word. This should in no way diminish the power or truth of what is communicated or its relevance to the sitter, for the slightest thing can have the most profound effect. That is spirit law and spirit knows best!

The health condition and the nature of their passing is further offered as evidence of contact together with memory links, description, occupation, characteristics and so on. If the sitter cannot take information about the spirit's health condition and the nature of their passing, together with the other information, then how can they possibly take the message that is to follow, or believe their loved one has survived the death of the physical body?

Reason for Coming

At the first opportunity, spirits are often desperate to communicate back to us their survival into the next world and that they still take an active interest in what goes on with those they have left behind. The other reason is love, of course! That is why Beethoven and Elvis do not come through at sittings or clairvoyant demonstrations. Love is the universal law and unless that love bond is evident, people of that ilk will not come – they have no reason to. But when that connection is made to a loved one, a special power then begins to flow: comforting the bereaved, giving hope to the lonely and healing to their spirit. A good contact always includes the spirits relaying *why* they have come through. So having laid the groundwork by providing much of the preceding information; in effect opening the door, the message now stands on a solid, firm foundation.

A criticism often levelled at spiritual mediums concerns the messages they bring, which can seem mundane to the observer. But there is a reason for this and it is to do with psychic science. A true spiritual medium knows you must take account of your own life; that is part of the function, code and philosophy of life on the earth plane and forms the discussion part of why we incarnate here. If this were not so then mediums would be constantly petitioned to give up six magic numbers each week. They would be telling people what house to buy, which holiday to go on and which relationship to make or break. That is not the way of the spirit and therefore not the way of the spirit medium.

Tidy Up

The good news the recipient should be left with is the truth they are not alone; that someone cares and they are only a thought away. The medium will finish with something that inspires the recipient into a deeper thinking about where they are on their path. As a result of the communication, they should be better empowered to make the right decisions at the right time and for the right reasons. All spirits need do is let us know they are there and are concerned for us. They do not frighten or alarm us and warnings, when given, are softened with a smile.

Using the Psychic Faculty in a Reading

Jesus often used psychic power to rekindle faith in an individual. For example, the woman of Samaria at Jacob's well (St. John 4. 10–29). Wearied by his journey, Jesus sends his disciples off into the city to buy food. A woman then arrives to draw water and he knows by intuition he can change her into an instrument of sovereign and divine will. He asked her to fetch her husband to which she replied she had no husband. Psychically well aware of this, he turned to her, now she had passed his little *truth* test, and said, *'You have had five husbands. The one you are with now you are not married to.'* This was purely psychic and it got her thinking. *'Sir, I perceive that thou art a prophet,'* she replied. And by the time the disciples returned to him, she had left for the city to tell all who would listen, *'Come, see a man that has told me all the things that I ever did!'*

This has got to be the oldest recorded (and most amazing) private sitting of all time! Spiritual mediums know, as Jesus did, that there is nothing like faith to boost psychic power. He used this psychic power to set ablaze the spark of faith contained within her. (If you read the full extract, you will note how Jesus succeeds in breaking through the taboos of sexism and racism.) Let this example also be an instrument in your diagnostic toolbox.

Mechanics or Science of Mediumship: How Does it Work?

When we learn to drive a car, through our five main senses, we are at first bombarded with an overload of information to the conscious mind. We are fearful of our position on the road, our speed, the various gauges, our mirrors, other road users, the gear we have selected and so on. But after a while these things go into the subconscious, and with adequate practice we find we can happily drive the vehicle whilst talking to our passengers, listening to the radio and thinking about what we are going to do when we get there. In other words, with time, these things are absorbed into the unconscious and become second nature.

Conversely, the spirit works in reverse. They get in touch with our subconscious mind by contacting the inspirational and creative part of the brain. This communication then manifests itself through any one of the five senses, i.e. we get tastes, aromas, we see, hear and feel them. The accessing of this area of the mind by spirits means it can be easy for the novice to confuse that which comes from within with that which comes from without. Is it imagination or is it a genuine communication? So how do we know the difference? *Practice!* The musician has the gift, but it needs development. The artist has the gift, but it needs development.

EXERCISE

Let us create an ideal template sitting for the novice medium in the circle, awareness class or one-to-one. Remember, everything is a communication from the moment you start working.

You stand up to show you are working. You may or may not have anything in your mind when you do so, but that is not important at this stage. If not already impinged upon then try to sense where you are drawn. Once you have identified a likely candidate, if possible, try to stand in their aura field. All five senses come stronger into play when this happens. With the sitter, you see a mental picture in your mind of, let us say, a rose. So you give out a rose. The rose on its own means nothing so you feel you have failed and sit down wondering why you bothered in the first place, or what on earth you were doing thinking you could be a medium. But before you sat, perhaps you felt dizzy and a tension in your heart area. Possibly the pressure was more than you could bear and this mental feeling of giving up became your reason? But if everything is a communication then perhaps you need to look again.

As with scrying and other discerning exercises, you must be greedy and scramble for every scrap they give you. What if you were told that what you had just been given was as much as any medium? And that you failed only because you did not know how to interpret and articulate the vast amount of information given to you in that moment? Strange as this may sound, experience tells us that even an accomplished medium receives no less and no more than the fledgling. But through experience they learn to decode and extract from the inspired clue. As with so many other things, it is one per cent inspiration, ninety-nine per cent perspiration.

Look again at the rose. What colour is it? Does it have thorns and if so, are they to harm or protect? And whom are they harming or protecting? Is the rose passed its best or is it yet to come to full bloom? Perhaps it is at full bloom now? Are there tears with this rose and if so are they happy or sad? Is it for a memory, an anniversary or perhaps a passing? Is the rose from a loved one in spirit, or is it for someone close to the recipient? Is there a name associated with the rose? Perhaps the rose itself is a communicating spirit's name. You will not know any of this for sure until you ask. All that from a rose!

These conversations with yourself, in time, will happen in a fraction of a second. The spirits are extremely economic with what they give out, meaning the novice receives no more than the adept. They will not waste time telling you or the sitter things you already know unless it is pertinent to conditions existing around the reading.

The tightness or pressure around the heart, together with the feeling of giving up, could be a message about how the spirit felt prior to passing. So perhaps they passed with a heart condition. Perhaps you mistook your own nervousness for that of the spirit's. They blended with you and by doing so brought their health and emotional condition with them, which through inexperience and lack of confidence, you interpreted it as being your own. You took on their emotions, albeit briefly. It lifted once you sat down and broke the communication.

Let us suppose you stand back up because now you have a name in your head and you are certain it is Rose. (See how economic the spirits can be with their information?) It does not matter at this stage whether the recipient can take the message – you must carry on. Many times people have come back later and verified a name. So what of this name? How does it connect? Is it in the family or a friend? If in the family, which side – father or mother's? If it is a friendship connection then how will the sitter know them? Perhaps they were a neighbour, work colleague or someone with whom they went to school.

All that from a name! As written in Chapter Three, a picture can be put into your mind by the spirit and it is up to you to translate and communicate its meaning. Sometimes the novice (like Jesus at the well) will begin on a psychic link as a way into the spirit connection. This is quite common and should not be frowned upon.

Remember we said you must be greedy? That includes using all the techniques at your disposal because now you are standing up again, you have accepted everything as a possible communication. So, you suddenly find yourself looking at the drapes. Why? What have they to do with anything? Perhaps the recipient is contemplating a purchase or has already parted with money for a set. Maybe this symbolises more light needed in the home or privacy. Maybe this is represents a house they visit where help is needed. But let us say that if the drapes should refer to the recipient directly, then the spirit is letting them know by this type of allusion that they are aware of their thoughts and concerns in the mundane. And should the recipient have recently acquired a set of these, then most likely the spirit would have been present in the store with them the day they were purchased.

So, as you can see, you may find yourself scrying a message from items and things surrounding you at the time of reading. Do not shut this down. The economy of spirit means they sometimes impinge upon you to decode their messages through that which is immediately visible to you. It is vitally important you find your own unique communication code. This means building a psychic and mental library of pictures, symbols, feelings, words and so much more.

Another thing you will notice is mediums often describing someone in great detail, which can be very impressive. But do not be fooled into thinking they are looking at an almost photo-graphic mental image (as some would have you believe). That degree of realism is either psychic or simply very rare, and when it does occur it is for a very particular reason not told here. For the most part, mental imagery is used for communication evinced when the medium is shown a photograph of the person they have just described. They will not recognise them save by instinct! Why? Because the spirits deal in symbols, representation and caricature.

Let us say the medium has described a girl child. The medium will have merely seen a representation of a girl child and not a photographic image. The representation can be a far more accurate tool for description than a photograph when it comes to articulating a description to a third party. So, when the medium says the child wore a yellow dress, white shoes and had blond bunches, they were seeing and interpreting a version of a yellow dress, shoes and hair on a representative child figure. What they saw (and said) was most likely not the *reality* in terms of the girl's graphic style and look. But by describing the child this way, the recipient was immediately able to accept what was offered because it fitted with their version, recollection or knowledge of the child in question. It is not a trick, but a brutal and honest appraisal of the gift. This is the way spirit work for the majority of time. By saying otherwise denies not only the truth but helps maintain the sad divorce either wilfully or ignorantly kept in place by those who seek to keep this knowledge secret. The reality of spirit communication should be truthfully and freely shared with all people.

Neither is there a 'telephone conversation' going on between the medium and the spirit. This is a fallacy designed to impress a gathering as to the sincerity and nature of the communication. Mediums hear clairaudiently to the rear of the physical ear or mentally in the mind like a voice in the head. Voices heard this way are always sweet and serene in nature and carried on a special wave of energy.

Chapter Fifteen

Healing: What It is and How to Do It

From spirit – to spirit – through spirit

What we are discussing here is spiritual and psychic healing of the mind, body and spirit. It can be applied to relationships, children, animals, plants and the earth. In fact there are no limits to healing power. As with clairvoyance, it is the total giving over of oneself as the instrument. Healing through the aura, healing by the laying on of hands or contact healing, and remote, distance or absent healing are what concern us here.

To heal is to restore and though this may not always be possible, students would do well to remember that the healing intelligence influences all you do in this field. A knowledge of anatomy, although desirable, is not a prerequisite.

Healing is a form of mediumship. Whilst it is true to say that all spiritual mediums are healers, not all spiritual mediums are better healers than those dedicated to the practice. It operates on a much slower vibration than clairvoyance. Its effects can be long lasting and life changing. It is not supernatural; it is supernormal.

You may scarce need reminding that healing practice is far more prevalent than is generally realised. We see examples of this in our lives daily. For instance, when a child is injured, the parent will automatically place their hand to the point of pain and give a gentle reassurance to the child that they are concerned and care. These are the ways in which we all heal and are done without thought or question. It is a natural human reaction.

Spiritual Healer, Harry Edwards, (1893–1976) stated that healing cannot be developed in the same way as the arts and sciences. Neither can it be bestowed by a degree, an ordination or the wearing of special garments. He said it functions when those who possess the healing ability establish contact with, and attune themselves to the source, including the 'intelligent administrators of this beneficial power'.

When you heal there are literally hundreds of spirits working through you. Therefore you cannot claim it as your own or allow others to think you are the source of the power you channel. You heal through the aura and the healing energy (by intelligence) is directed to where it is needed. You do not have to actually place your hands over an affected area of the body, especially if that hand placement may cause embarrassment. However, it is noted that some people do express a preference for the healer's hands to be placed over an affected area. This can boost the patient's confidence that healing is actually taking place. You, as the instrument, may also be guided that way too. Concerning privy parts and the like, healers should naturally refrain from contact with these areas. A modicum of commonsense would be prudent. For example, a woman's chest can be healed through the back.

By healing, you receive healing too. Do not try to direct it yourself otherwise you may end up drained. It is also worth noting that some healers may themselves have long term illnesses and disabilities. This forms part of the criticism of healing practice and it is easy to see why. After all, if they are such good healers, how come they have not been able to heal themselves? But it is not as simple as 'physician heal thyself'. There are many theories out there, but the true nature of illness, its causes or remedy are still relatively unknown. All you need know is that spiritual healing works, always has and always will.

For all the good it does, the medical profession and Big Pharma are one of the most consummate killers on the planet. So do not be distracted by the arguments of practitioners and non-believers who will try to persuade you what you are doing is causing harm or is nothing more than fakery or psychic quackery. Be strong and remember you are reawakening that which has lain suppressed in you (and humankind) for so long.

Unlike clairvoyance, the quality of the healing does not rely on you not knowing the recipient. Whether they are family, friend or stranger, the healing power goes to where it is needed most. Over time, and repeated sessions, you begin to build-up a rapport with your patient. You may be their only source of comfort. Children and animals respond particularly well. Spiritual healer, Tom Johansen, once said, 'Just wanting to help someone is the highest form of prayer.' The medical profession grudgingly acknowledges the psychological aspects to this work but not the physical.

Healing the soul can affect the body and vice versa. For example, a bad person who receives spiritual healing may benefit on a physical level. This can affect them on a spiritual level and they may find themselves now inspired into deeper thinking about this *strange* power. It could herald the dawn of a new light within them.

Magnetic Healing

So called because of how it feels as it flows through the body. In common with all life forms, the human body has strong electro-magnetic properties. We are transceivers, which means, we transmit and receive energy. Orgone energy, as discovered by Wilhelm Reich (1897–1957), may explain this better, together with other studies on the subject such as Dr Oz or the Kirlian Effect. Note also the work being done in the re-emergence of diamag-netism and its effect and levitation of water molecules in the human body.

The healer may experience a magnetic rocking sensation in the body as well as a pulling energy surrounding the arms extending down to the hands. This force is intelligently controlled and directed and you should allow it to move freely though you.

The Laying On of Hands – Contact Healing

It is not unusual for the healer to make some form of initial contact with the patient. This may take the form of holding their hands or placing hands on their shoulders. This is part of the blending process. Keep it simple and sincere. If you observe a healing group at work, it may look like contact but often their hands are off the body by a small degree.

Equipment

A comfortable armless chair and or portable medical bed, a bowl of warm water, a towel, some handkerchiefs and drinking water are really all you need.

The ambience can be enhanced by candles and appropriate music but this is not essential or required and may be a distraction if perfumed or smoky and the music too loud or not to the taste of the recipient. The armless chair allows all round access and in the case of the patient's back, they can simply turn to the side giving ease of exposure. A bed offers other options in terms of all round access to the anatomy. The towel and water are in the interests of hygiene, though not essential, and can be used as a break between treatments if there is more than one patient. Handkerchiefs are for tears. Sometimes this happens when a person comes for healing. Tears are a good indication of the soul being healed.

EXERCISE
Healing Through the Aura

The Patient

Sit opposite your patient and begin an informal conversation centred around ascertaining their reasons for wanting healing. Make sure you explain there are no guarantees involved in what you do. Also point out that if they are under a doctor they should continue to seek their services. By offering them healing, you are not a replacement for a medical practitioner. It is a good idea to state that when they come to you for healing, they do so entirely of their own volition. All they need do is sit for you. You are unlikely to touch them.

How to Heal

Stand behind your patient with your hands at your side. Take several controlled deep breaths. Slowly lift your hands up to cover their shoulders – all the time sensing for external intelligent control. For a few brief seconds, allow your hands to rest on their shoulders. Now lift your hands off an inch or two and spend a few moments blending and sensing the layers and interplay of the aura. By doing this you are stimulating and attuning yourself to ever finer degrees and linking with the patient's condition.

To heal in this position may be all you are inspired to do – nothing more. On the other hand you may feel you are pulled and guided to move around the patient while the spirit seeks to find a better focus point for the rays. At this moment you are under their control. You operate in a form of very light trance. You may feel you should keep your fingers closed or open. You may feel one hand is a stronger channel than the other. These are all things for you to explore and decide – we are all unique.

When you feel the time is right, return, if possible, to where you started with your hands over the shoulders of the patient. Gently rest your hands on them, thereby giving indication you have finished the session. Ask them how they feel and make sure they are okay. You and the patient may require a glass of water.

Duration

Most healings can be accomplished in 10 minutes. The longest is usually 20 minutes, though there are certain exceptions. Your individual patient healing sessions should be characterised by the former, not the latter.

Responses

Your heart may go out to a patient and you may think you are going to feel great energy only to find that what you felt fell way below your (usual) expectations. In these cases it is not out of the ordinary for the recipient to turn to you and say that was the most powerful feeling they have ever experienced! Sometimes this works the other way too, so be warned.

Sometimes a patient will place great faith in you and you may seem unable, or unmoved, to make a connection that would warrant such belief they have in you. In these cases do not worry – you are, as always, only the instrument. Sometimes when you are healing you will find yourself thinking of the most mundane things such as your shopping list or that odd job that needs doing at home. Do not see this as a lack of discipline or failure to focus on your part. And do not see it either as meaning the healing power is diminished for your lack of mental attention. Some of the most powerful healings delivered have been achieved in this 'off line' frame of mind. Again, *you* are merely the instrument.

Terminal Illness

People will come to you as a last resort in many cases. You are then expected to produce a miracle cure. And when and if they pass, people will criticise you and what you do as nothing more than useless and giving false hope. But so-called 'miracles' do happen all the time and when they do, the same people are quick to point out that it was the doctor or a drug that really did it. But if you truly work in the light you will know when divine power has intervened and in many cases so will the patient.

The Nature of Healing

In the Bible there are many examples of healing by Jesus. Whether you believe in it or not is irrelevant. As a student and practitioner of psychic science you would do well to be interested in some of the very clear laws it reports as happening with regard to healing. For instance, when Jesus healed the ten lepers, only one returned to give him thanks, to which Jesus is recorded as saying, 'Your faith has made you whole.' So we know the other nine were not changed by the experience, save in the flesh. Whereas the one that returned received healing in mind, body and spirit. Like Jesus, sometimes your healing may only work on the physical.

Look at the story of the woman with an issue of blood who knew that if she could but touch the hem of the garment of Jesus then she would be healed throughout. In this case there was a multitude around him so her task was made all the more difficult. Nonetheless she managed to touch his hem. At that moment he at once turned and asked, 'Who touched me?' They replied that they were all touching him. 'No,' he said, 'one of you has touched me.' Concerned by all the fuss, the woman spoke up and said, 'It was I.' Then a very interesting exchange takes place between Jesus and the woman in which she explains that she has had the condition twelve years and had spent everything on physicians until she had nothing left. Then he tells her that her faith has made her complete.

Faith is here defined as meaning to actively believe. The question is, did Jesus heal or was it her belief in his ability to heal? Was Jesus merely the instrument? The answer is somewhere between the two. As you heal, people will come to believe you can heal them when sometimes all you are doing is nothing more than the laying on of hands. When you are experienced enough, you will come to know of this story's veracity, because on occasion, by the merest touch, you will feel what Jesus felt, described in the Bible as 'knowing in himself that virtue had gone out of him'.

It is oftentimes reported that Jesus told those healed to tell no one. Why? He knew of the fragility of human faith and that there were many who would seek to undermine the great work achieved bringing about a cure. The world is full of people quick to destroy the good done by the spirit. 'Keep it to yourself', he would tell them, for this and no other reason.

Remote, Distance or Absent Healing

Keep your own healing list and browse it from time to time. Tell people you will add them to it. If it is a public list then keep their condition private. Distance is no barrier to the healing power. If you would like to give someone healing without their permission – perhaps they are antagonistic towards the process, then simply send out your healing thoughts as if they were physically there with you. Unlike aura and auragraph readings, it is not an invasion of privacy. By doing this you are breaking no code. Strange as it may seem, you may be pleasantly surprised to find them seeking you out for healing one day! Sit back from afar and watch the spirit work on them. Either way, just do what is required and seek no reward or recognition because you are operating on a higher vibration. Keep it pure. Self is enemy to the process.

EXERCISE
A Dowsing by Hand Exercise for the Awareness Class

This is a great way to learn to use your hands as carriers and sensors of healing energy. The patient can either sit, stand or lie. Stand aside them and guide your hands over their body, usually six to twelve inches away. What you are looking for are changes in heat, magnetism and the like. You may be drawn to a point and feel you have to stop. Ask the patient if they have a complaint there. If they do then well done! If they do not then it can simply indicate a change in the aura field. It is amazing what you can pick up this way. As a rule, refrain from diagnosing.

X-ray Vision

As you dowse and become more familiar with the practice of healing, you may become aware of pictures in your mind appearing to show you bones, nerves, organs and the like. This is perfectly normal. The ancient shamans were able to visualise through the human body to a point of pain, disease and disorder, helping them bring about amazing cures and reliefs. You may also begin to mentally image the auras and chakras at will. By doing this you are simply re-awakening an ability within you which brings its own rewards.

Creating Healing Water

Use filtered water for the best results. Whether in a group or on your own, place your hands around a body of water and heal it in the same way you would a person. The healing intelligence will tell you when to stop. Once charged, the water can be stored and consumed at leisure. It can also be diluted to share amongst others, particularly your patients. This is a great way to get a boost into your biological system. Take a little sip each day and feel the benefit. Offer it to your patients. The truth about water is slowly coming about. It is the most amazing substance we have on the planet! For further study, investigate 'water memory'.

Certification, Recognition and Healing Insurance

You are born free, you live free and you 'die' free! So, feel free to ignore self-appointed bodies for spiritual healing, offering 'certification', 'recognition', and 'healing insurance'. The law, as it stands, is more than adequate to deal with any cases of abuse (which are unlikely to arise) or for that which may be deemed inappropriate. Provided you have not committed a criminal or common law offense, then you need not consent or respond to any statute, act, regulation or rule, i.e. civil matter. Remember, as stated above in 'The Patient', people have come to you of their own volition. Always have a third party present if that makes things easier for you and all concerned. And that is all you need.

Jesus, Moses, Mohammed, St Francis and even Harry Edwards, did not require pieces of paper to do what they did.

These organisations (who upon proper construction are found to be predatory by nature) have but one master, which, like Hydra, are possessed of five heads – *money, power, fear, greed* and *control*. They each make a profit, irrespective of what their non-profit legal company status appears to be. If that were not so, would they do it free? Between them they seem to want to regulate and organise healing as if it were a commodity to be bought, sold and licensed. For money, they offer courses and membership subscriptions. They use fear to blackmail people and organisations (often by attrition) into thinking they need to be covered for doing something as natural as breathing! Some people want to belong to these self-appointed bodies and that is their right. But it is not solely the right of the same to be the only ones allowed to heal. They seek (blind as they are) to control that which is free to all. But they cannot command the power of the spirit any more than you can.

They will tempt you into contracting with them for years to become something that literally takes *minutes* to learn, by offering you a piece of paper with a name, date and seal that you can stick on a wall somewhere! As Jesus said, 'They have their reward.' This book is a challenge to those organisations who seek to keep this knowledge secret.

Should you ever feel unsafe conducting a healing session then simply exercise your right to say no. You need not explain your reasons. *No* is the most powerful word we have yet we seldom use it. Offer absent or distance healing as an alternative. Remember, you are sovereign in these matters.

Chapter Sixteen

Protection

Let that which is within you rise up and be your protection

This is a very misunderstood category of psychic and spiritual awareness. There are techniques available for protection, but before we come onto that, perhaps we need to ask something of ourselves first. From whom, what and why do you need this protection? What is it you think is most likely going to happen to you? For the most part the resounding answer to this will be *nothing*. Because as you progress to ever higher vibrations of thought, you will realise that protection, outside of the physical world, is nothing more than a frame of mind and spiritual consciousness.

If you follow the examples shown in this volume, the protection you seek will go with you automatically. It is installed free with the application, so to speak. This book is both a diagnostic instrument and toolbox. *You* are your own protection. However, if you think there is some magic formula that will give you an exemption from attack when you undertake this work then you are seriously mistaken and perhaps need to stop what you are doing now. There is an old saying adopted by Spiritualists the world over, *'Fear the living: not the dead'*. But whilst nothing will happen to you, attacks will occur as you engage, and are engaged by, discarnate entities from realms hidden from our sight by the thinnest of veils. This may sound contradictory, but both points are true. For this work requires the fighter in you to come out and to challenge as well as defend. Not one beacon for light and truth gone before us was ever passive! We have dominion over the earth plane surface and we have control over ourselves – we *are* the control. Realising this means you have already won!

As discussed in *Meditation*, without control of mind you cannot control your wanderings and neither can you control your experiences should they become strong to you. Burning a few herbs will do nothing and it is sad that many people are still beholding to what we shall call hocus pocus, voodoo and other such psychic quackery. How can things made of atoms and molecules be required to ameliorate and temperance that which is of the spirit? Evil, when reflected back to its source, like the flame of a candle in a looking glass, cannot harm the mirror. These things only have the power you or the recipient give them. They are illusions of the mind. It is true some mischievous spirits access our world through the human mind (of the less strong) leading them to believe they are possessed, when in reality they are obsessed. This whole book is a protection in itself.

EXERCISE
Novices and fledglings may like to try the following very simple technique as they try to find their feet in this new world opened to them. In its uncomplicated form, choose either violet or pink and place it like a bubble around yourself and the dwelling, the place or the person you want to protect. This can be very effective (see Chapter Six).

This high colour works by insulating you from being affected by, or taking on the jaded, low and negative aura energies, emotional conditions and fatigue associated with troubled spirits. It enables you to be a non-affected participant observer. You must decide for yourself how much you want to get involved, but the mechanism, once put in place, is there if it should be required. It also works with the 'living' too. If you are exposed to any situation where you are weary of contact, such as counselling a client or going to a home where stress and fatigue vibrations dominate, apply the exercise before entering therein. Note that upon leaving, and for the time thereafter, you will feel no after effect almost irrespective of what you may have encountered there.

You will often hear of people being 'psychically attacked' by another. Again, this has no more power than the alleged victim affords it. And as for those who partake in such extremes and nonsense, the only achievement for them is the destruction of their own soul.

Chapter Seventeen

Rescue Work

Passed over souls who are closer to the earth plane than the spirit world

If you are of a clairvoyant disposition, from time to time you may be called upon to 'exorcise' a 'ghost' that is reported to you as causing trouble at a place of dwelling. There are reckoned to be mediums who specialise in this area of spirit rescue, but upon its proper construction, being a spiritual *medium* presupposes your ability to ameliorate this situation without hindrance. Again, psychic science will be your guide. Take a good, experienced spiritual healer with you if possible, though this is not always necessary, for the true spiritual medium is both healer and rescuer. Healers *can* do this work alone, but will be unable converse with the spirit one-to-one.

Firstly, always look for the rational explanation to what is happening. Sometimes a client may be lonely and seeking attention. They could have mental problems or be prone to creative and wild exaggerations. Whatever way you look at it, it still requires a consummate medium to diagnose the problem. From the first point of contact with the person your instincts will tell you of your involvement or if it is a hoax. Set your stall out early: this means 'calling out' the person reporting the phenomena if you think it bogus or fantasised.

Assuming you are given notice, say a day or more before beginning your investigation, you should start sending out healing and rescue thoughts to all those concerned in this scenario, as well as the location. Using an inbuilt remote viewing technique, some mediums find it helpful to study an aerial map of the site if they are unfamiliar with its geography. You should ask for empowering help, not only from your spirit guides, friends and helpers, but also from those on the other side associated with both the client and the spirit involved. So as you can see, when you embark on this work, in partnership with you, a whole team is involved helping a troubled spirit 'across'. The spirit world cannot always do this work alone. Why? Because discarnate spirits are often closer to the earth plane than to the spirit world.

Rescue work falls into a number of basic categories. In a hypothetical house-haunting scenario, a family are disturbed by the following:

The Recording, Time Echo or Stone Tape Theory

The family home is centuries old. It does not have to originally been a home. It may have been built for some other purpose and at some point in its history has been converted. The materialised, or moderately materialised, form of a woman appears around the area of (let us say) the kitchen. Furthermore, she appears to be floating somewhat off the floor, or perhaps part way through it. She is dressed in medieval clothing and seems oblivious to the present incumbents, even when appearing in front of them. Experience tells us that what the family is witnessing is a replay of something that happened a long time ago. The spirit of the woman is no longer there, but whatever happened to her in that house has left a deep and lasting psychic imprint that has remained an active energy far beyond her earthly time.

In cases like these, one or more of the family members are often found to have mediumistic abilities. This is an important point because it can have the effect of amplifying the phenomena all the more. Another contributory factor could be the site of the home on a ley line. In these circumstances there is very little that can be done outside of re-pointing the carrier channel (impossible if it is a primary ley).

A spirit will only haunt a location for usually no more than six generations after its passing. Beyond that they are naturally moved on by the spirit world. And because we know this is true we can therefore determine that should the family report the spirit as looking straight at them or interacting with them in some way, they are simply triggering the experience by virtue of being in the right spot at the right time. This maybe a bed, a chair or standing somewhere in the house pertinent to the apparition's traumatic history. For the spectator, this has no more significance than when a character in a film looks directly into the lens. It may seem they are looking straight at you, but space and time separate both subject and voyeur. You can see them, but they cannot see you. The place of its occurrence would be considered a hotspot. The appearance off or through the floor can be explained by its height differing in their time to where it is now. In these cases, an investigation into the history of the house should be undertaken.

Poltergeist Activity

This area forms part of what is called physical phenomena and, amongst other things, includes levitation, apparitions, objects moved through space and time, and the creation of ectoplasm. Strangely, of the objects that can appear, some may have belonged to the incumbent family from their past. This part of the activity remains unexplained. However, the majority of materialisations *will* be to do with the discarnate spirit exclusively and can be a mixture of items from the contemporary house and the era from which the spirit hails. These so-called apports should be taken as a form of communication.

In our preferred case, the family have a female child reaching the age of puberty, around whom the psychic and physical energies centre. As to exactly why children of this age should be the focus of attention is another mystery, though a number of theories abound.

Poltergeists can be spirits who may or may not be aware they have passed over. This is discussed in Chapter Nineteen. Nonetheless, of their conscious or unconscious volition, they can create mischief and mayhem. Poltergeists who have become aware of their condition and circumstance will have most likely refused to go to the light at the time of their passing. This can be for any number of reasons such as misdemeanours committed when alive in the physical world, mental illness or non-belief and acceptance of a life after death. They become restless and earth-bound in a dream state through the shear terror and frustration of seeking to escape an inevitable fate that awaits them on the other side – a world they have created for themselves! Their relatives and those they knew when on earth will eventually come to their rescue. But sometimes these things cannot wait. This is where the spiritual rescue medium comes in.

Do not underestimate the power of a poltergeist to terrify and cause disruption or the influence of their negative, overbearing energy that can saturate a place or situation. They feed off emotions and the subconscious. You will often find that families afflicted by such will frequently be in emotional conflict themselves. They can also charm pets and children, so be aware. In the worst cases, poltergeist activity can cause what is known as elemental damage such as flooding or fire, as well as problems to electrical systems because of their electromagnetic strength. This latter symptom is extremely rare. Do not play with these spirits as they already exist in a delusional state. They can also access our world through the human mind, so be aware of their power to manipulate. Unless they are put to rest by an experienced medium, the disturbances will continue. If the spirit forms an attachment to an individual in the family, let us say the girl, and the family move location, the spirit can follow.

Additional Examples

Now all this may sound frightening and you may feel powerless to do anything against such extremes. However, as a true worker in the field, you will know that we, the flesh and blood human beings, have dominion over the earth plane surface – something we sometimes forget. For all their terror, their removal can be quite simple and effective, which we shall come to.

Sometimes a rescue is required where the use of a Ouija board has attracted earthbound souls. There is nothing wrong with a Ouija board, however, you may be surprised to learn that very few people actually know how to use one. This knowledge should remain secret because in the wrong hands it can lead to mental breakdown and paranoia in the inexperienced.

When rescuing, the personal circumstances of the client should be taken into account. No matter how gifted, always be careful what you get yourself into. Some examples could be, say, a passed over relative who has not made a good transition or is still somehow emotionally bound to the conditions of the earth life they have left behind. There could be mistreatment of one or more children in the family home. Perhaps it is a long lost family member who was murdered or passed in unnatural circumstance and wants to bring attention to themselves and or the circumstances of their demise. Perhaps there is a deep (and emotionally scarring) split in a relationship that is giving concern to someone on the other side. Either way, every soul tells its own special story.

Some people consider their ghost to be 'friendly', and that may be so where a loved one wishes to make their presence known. But the rest are disturbed spirits, otherwise they would not be in this situation. What started off as a so-called friendly spirit, can quickly change to become a real nuisance. If the spirit is attached to the house then renovation or building work will heighten their activity in what they still see as their home and their exclusive possession. Where a haunting has occurred for a century or more it may be as well to note that the geography and the location has, most likely, remained unchanged since that time, thereby giving them a sense of familiarity and safety. From time to time we all experience a bad dream. Never lose sight of the fact that these discarnate souls often exist permanently in that type of nightmare state. That is what you are trying to communicate with, so how difficult is that going to be?

How to Rescue

First and foremost – you are the control! Taking onboard all we have just discussed, you should enter the location positive and ready to work. Do not do so if you are fatigued, suffering ill health or otherwise distracted. Remember, you are approaching this rescue without prejudice, so walk throughout the location without being swayed or overly influenced by testimony and history. Your magnetic and emotional aura fields will inform you where the hotspots of activity loom. See if this concords with the client's version. But whether it does or not is neither here nor there, for you are the instrument, there to diagnose and repair. As a mindset, this will characterise your work here. Your faith and confidence should be in no doubt. Though not necessarily an absolute requirement, the client's confidence in your ability will only help.

Decide what it is you can feel. Is it magnetic or physical or is it purely emotional such as fear, loss, or depression? It may be a combination of both. But in reality, you need not do anything other than turn up at the location because when you are working properly; when you are following the laws, the rest will be done for you by the spirit world. You will instantly become aware of the energy and presence filling the place. You will say your own invocation and communicate with the discarnate spirit by letting them know you are there to free them from their bondage to their nightmare state. 'It's over', 'Time to move on', 'Go to the light', 'See your family calling you – listen to them', and other imperatives should be employed by you from the heart.

Put yourself in their position. Imagine, if you will, you are dreaming and someone continually comes to you telling you that you are dead. A tunnel of light appears which frightens you because you know that to enter therein means there will be no return. Who wants to be dead, right? It goes against every natural instinct we have. This person seems to have a power to force you to accept something you cannot believe in. All you want to now do is go home where you feel safe and secure. But when you get there, strangers are moving in and changing all your things. You try to stop them but to no avail. So the nightmare continues. To make matters worse, they seem ignorant of your presence. And just like in a dream, there is no sense of time passing. A century may seem like a week.

This is what you, the medium, are up against. This is why healing forms an integral part of what you do. You will also need to draw on your capacity for compassion and understanding. Add to that your faith, i.e. that you actively believe in what you are doing. You are dealing with mentally disturbed spirits. But once you begin to move them on, you will experience an exhilarating or uplifting feeling. This hidden work you do forms a very important part of mediumship per se. Following a successful rescue, the spirit will at some point return to you to give thanks.

Remember that after moving the spirit on, latent psychic imprints will still be left at the location forming part of its history. Post rescue, clients may return to you informing you of the phenomena's return. Maybe a psychic has told them this and it will be mistakenly picked up as failure on your part – so be aware. The client needs to be told this. Once it has gone, it has gone for good. Little, however, can be done about the history.

Rescue Circle

If this class of spirit work interests you then the formation of a rescue circle may be in order. It follows the rules and guidance for all circles and meditation, albeit with a slightly different remit. The variation here is that the active part of the circle will request the spirit world to bring to the circle souls who simply do not know they have passed. In an hour of sitting it is possible to rescue several souls, though not at the same time, for each must be given sufficient undivided attention so as to ensure a successful transition to the higher side. The composition of the circle requires the spiritual medium, one or more healers, though not essential, and other like-minded people willing to give of their time to sit and devote their energy. A circle scribe may be in order to log and track the information exchanged in the circle. The medium concerned should inform the circle with a commentary of what is happening and inform them aloud of any mental questions asked and answers received.

Visitations Whilst Asleep

These can be very distressing, even for the most experienced medium because they are brought to you when you are in an altered or lucid dream state. Your defences can be greatly weakened but this can be necessary when it comes to dream rescue because unless your firewall is down, they cannot get through. This is always done by prior agreement and a conscious or unconscious consent on your part with those in the spirit world. In other words, this is what you have agreed to so do not complain when they come calling at 3.15am. Also, spirits brought to you this way are every so often beyond the help of other types of rescue work. Sometimes you need to be on a level footing with the spirit you are rescuing and that can mean that you both meet on the astral plane with intercessors waiting in the wings to help.

Inter-dimensional Entities, ETs and Demons

As Hamlet says, 'There are more things in heaven and earth, Horatio, than are dreamt of in your philosophy.' From time to time, if you are so constituted, you will become aware of intelligences that appear to be not of this world or the next. Caution is strongly advised as they can be super intelligent deceivers. Only a fool would ignore the vast body of teachings and testimony from days of old where these special classes of contact are well documented. But as stated before, we (organic humans) have dominion over the (organic) earth surface. Strength of mind can easily repel (should they be) unwanted intrusions of this type.

Chapter Eighteen

Being a Worker in the Field for Spirit

Some tips and hints

This chapter deals with some of the philosophical points referred to in many of the other chapters. It is intended to give you an added perspective and is in no way without flaw, alteration or question. It is designed simply to inspire you into a deeper thinking about the spirit path and is organically linked to the topics herein.

As a worker in the field you will need to be articulate about some of the big fundamental questions when tackled, as well as for your own benefit generally. For the most part, orthodox religions ignore key questions about the nature of 'being' in a spiritual universe. They are less inclined to define in easy terms what it is like to tread an earthly path without resorting to scripture or flawed, indoctrinated philosophies that appear to put us at odds with that which has created us. For example, the idea that there is somehow a divorce in place between heaven and earth and that spiritual gifts can only be ministered and manifested through extreme devotion to some male dominated belief system. With the exception of what we shall term Natural Spiritualism, almost all religions are male dominated patriarchs insisting on some kind of abstinence, celibacy and or ceremony revering a deity. Their architected spirituality is based upon mantras that quickly dissolve when confronted. And those religions who offer an attempt at addressing these fundamentals of human life do so hiding behind trite phrases and pseudo-spiritual verbiage that speaks only to itself. They seldom, if ever, see the next world as anything other than a place of reward and punishment and they seem to take great pleasure in the unproven tenet that 'lost souls' will be destroyed by fire in misery and torment for all eternity. This is not your way to a spiritual unfolding or enlightenment. You do not have to go to India and sit in an Ashram for ten years! You can do it here and now. You are a living spirit with unlimited potential. For we know that which created us, and all we perceive, is not punitive but is instead filled with unlimited love.

We are not born in sin and neither are we flawed and require saving. We are not lost. God, if you like, is not human. A human could not have created all we experience. It is beyond human consciousness to comprehend let alone create all we know! We should not define God for anyone other than ourselves. So be free and let others be free also in what they believe. If all these male dominated (some exclusively) belief systems in the world are so great and have such a beautiful and powerful message for us, why will they not coexist with each other?

As an apprentice you must never go out to evangelise. People find their own way and will walk their own path. Remember, those shackled to dogma, creed and religion are at a place where perhaps you once resided. They are unlikely to have been where you are at this moment. You will sometimes meet aggression, shear belligerence or arrogance on the part of a questioner. In these cases you should always meet them with firmness and strength of character. A true worker will always know who is and who is not beyond their help. And that the latter may only be so presently. You should retreat with dignity and hope and pray that your fellow natural human being may one day become a more enlightened one.

It is said that when the true spirit light of awakening strikes even the darkest soul it shines all the more brightly for the sake of that darkness! So resist the temptation to judge those you may consider to be dwelling in darkness. Sometimes you will find darkness all around you and you will question the path. You will have difficulty reconciling the material world with all its pressures and complex problems with that of the spirit, where everything seems so simple and righteous. Do not let these things upset you. Your light is set amongst the dark – how else is it to be seen? What candle stands out in a room full of candles? And remember, you are equal to all the challenges placed before you. This is the way.

A true worker in the field will not be offended by the source of any knowledge, wisdom or teaching and neither will they see its spreading as an attempt to evangelise. Put simply, it is said the spirit moves through all religions. Religion can be the mule that brings you to the door, but not necessarily the means by which you enter the house! And in the same way a plan precedes a building, Jesus, Moses, St Francis or Viracocha for that matter, would not have been able to manifest the power of the spirit the way they did unless they were psychic to begin with.

Do not be like some scholars on this road who reject outright and recoil at the merest mention of scriptures or the workings of the ancient prophets. Suffice to say, they have their path and you have yours. Instead, be open to the ancient wisdom that has come down to us in abundance from everywhere for they were far wiser in those so-called ancient times. The challenge for some lies in seeing things for what they are and removing the blinkers of orthodoxy from those very same writings. When you truly develop the spirit influence this will be revealed to you; sometimes with pain, but mostly with a gentle (and knowing) surprise of the kind that comes to those who wish no more than to see the real truth of what lays behind the mask of human pain and suffering.

We are not alone in this universe. You will see there is so much more to heaven the earth. There are many souls who dwell within the higher spheres of consciousness and who will reach out to those so constituted to carry their communication. *Forget* what you have been told, because on the path you will discover that all human life, all human construction is based on a lie – one that has been told for real since olden times. No, it is not *you* who are crazy!

Orthodoxy and those who follow it in all its forms will despise you! They will seek to tell you that what you are doing and what you believe will lead you to burn in hell for all eternity. But who wants to go to a world where we must accept a path at odds with what we really are and what we truly feel? At the same time, we must respect people who are passionate believers in their chosen religion for you will hear that many great and important works have been done by men and women driven by orthodox teaching. For example, many devoted followers of orthodox religions spend time with people unknown to them in hospitals and centres for caring looking after both convert and atheist alike. But equally, could not all these things have been achieved by the shear goodness of human nature without religion? *'I'm doing this because I believe in this God or that God!'* and so on. You, on the other hand, as a worker in the field, will do these things because you are a human being with human and spiritual qualities that far exceed those branded corporatized religions. People who do these good works in the name of their god or religion hope to be 'judged' favourably by an archaic system of reward and chastisement, little realising they are their own judge. They often desire praise from their chosen god in return. That is the way of true hell and damnation. This is not the path of psychic and spiritual awareness you tread!

Respect the good in people and not their badges or labels.

So what label do *you* have? The answer is simple – wear whatever you like. As long as you cause no loss, harm or damage to another soul then you will be some way along the path to developing a purer, richer gift of the spirit. This *must* come from the heart and *not* the ego! You cannot bargain with yourself? You are, always have been and always will be, your own arbiter. So be honest and humble and give no thought for what you might say for the words will be given to you at the appropriate time.

Chapter Nineteen

What Happens When We 'Die'?

The transition from the corporeal

So, what Happens When We 'Die'? Does anyone know exactly?

Have you noticed how inarticulate other religions suddenly become when you ask them the following question, *'What happens to the soul after the death of the physical body?'* Try it next time you are petitioned by someone who is determined to prove that they are right in what they believe and you are wrong or a devil worshipper. As workers in the field we seldom, if ever, use the following terms: *dead, death* or *die*. Instead, we prefer to use terms such as *passed over, passed,* or *transition*. We accept there is no such thing as death. Death implies cessation of all activity. In reality, they are more alive over there than they ever were here.

No matter what the circumstances of a passing, we only make our transition from the corporeal at the precise moment we are meant to. Although it is often said, *'they went before their time'*, *'it was an accident'* and *'it was not meant to be'*, these are mere figures of speech and carry little weight. The Old Testament is accurate in its assertion that a silver cord is attached to the spiritual counterpart of the human body and remains so all the days of our earthly life. Even when we dream or astral travel, this cord remains connected at the solar plexus. Once the silver cord is severed, it is cut for good and the spirit cannot return to the body anymore than a newborn baby can return to the womb. It is the spiritual umbilical cord. So dying is the moment at which *only* the earthly life ceases.

People pass in many different ways and circumstances so what follows in the next segment is, at best, a generalisation, but a coherent one. For the purposes of this exercise, we shall categorise death in two ways, the death of the good person and the death of the bad person.

The Good Person

When we leave our earthly life we go to a world we have made for ourselves. In its simplest form, this means that for someone who led a life characterised by dishonesty will find very little awaiting them on the other side. Equally, if they led a good life characterised by forgiveness and generosity, then they will find a world filled with great beauty and light.

It is still true to say we will always find a world of forgiveness and compassion awaiting us on the other side, but not everyone can see it for what it is. Many times people on their deathbed or in the hours immediately prior to passing, report seeing long lost loved ones around them, almost like a welcoming. Just prior to the silver cord being broken, it is said our life flashes before us. The soul then floats free from the corporeal body. We exit through the crown chakra. Once free of the body, we become omniscient in our observations of what is going on around us. Although testimony varies somewhat, it seems we next find ourselves in a tunnel, travelling apace 'toward the light'. Having successfully traversed this commonly reported tunnel experience, the next phase finds us in a place which could be described as a meeting dimension. It is not our final destination but a kind of reception level. Some have described it as a higher astral level or slightly lower level of the spirit realm. It is possible to access this level with the silver cord still attached. Many people have gone there and returned to tell the tale. There is also strong evidence and testimony that we dwell there approximately three earthly days, moving between the earth and the astral before moving on to the higher side – similar to the Risen Christ experience. No one is really sure why this is save perhaps for adjustment.

Some people have passed traumatically. Some people have

suffered great anxiety prior to passing. In these cases there are what we may call 'hospitals' and especially dedicated healing places and centres to handle such souls as these. Do not get these places mixed up with earthly hospitals. They have a similar 'healthcare' vibration, but are devoid of the paraphernalia associated with their earthly counterpart. Here, they will find pure healing and restoration at a level and pace they are ready for. However, not everyone needs this experience.

Many good people who have been atheistic, agnostic, humanist and the like, pass unable to accept the world in which they now find themselves in. But it is not long before the love of spirit guides, helpers, friends and loved ones lead them to the truth and reality of where they are.

The Bad Person: This section is closely related to Chapter Seventeen

Not all who make the transition to the other side find a world of love, light, truth, happiness and forgiveness. There are some extremely dark levels to the spirit realms where fear, intimidation and impending doom permeate every aspect of existence therein and from which, it appears, there is no escape. Those who dwell there do so by virtue of the life and choices they made when on the earth or through a succession of lives. We do not fully under- stand the nature of human choice and freewill and how it affects our lives in the hereafter, but suffice to say, every soul tells its own special story. So we do not judge. We trust they are there because, for want of a better reason, they have put themselves there. 'Good people' do not find themselves in such places anymore than do the souls of animals or children. It can take many earth centuries to come out from there. Some may choose, or be given, the opportunity to reincarnate in order to attempt to right the wrongs they have done. Strange as it may seem, others are happy to dwell there. These souls are clever but flawed by the evil that resides in their hearts. Until that is conquered, they will remain there for as long as it takes. Acceptance of their short-comings, misdemeanours and soul-set, accounts for the bulk of their journey along the road to self-salvation. The awesome problem of souls gone astray in a world of dread and fear is they also lack the imagination required to acknowledge what they have done.

Some have lived lives (perhaps several) where they have caused nothing but pain and misery to others. Some miscreant souls pass suddenly, either in sleep or through a collapse and find themselves in a strange new existence. They are outside their physical 'dead' body looking at themselves lying prostrate but unable to communicate with those on the earth. They are invisible and inaudible to people who are suddenly moving into their home and changing everything. In a mixture of anger, frustration and fear, they begin to cause psychic phenomena. This, if not rescued by an accomplished spiritual medium, can continue for many decades and cause no end of trouble for the people who come to dwell there after them (Chapter Seventeen).

As a walker of the path, you should endeavour to be the best that you can be. This does not mean living a life dreading some kind of divine retribution. We have no fear unless we invite it in. God, if you like, is not punitive. We are not born in sin. We need no redeemer or saviour to come to our rescue. As stated at the beginning of this work – you progress by your own efforts and are responsible for everything you do. So be good and act good on the part of genuine motive and greater works will follow you.

Chapter Twenty

'Addressing' Some Questions

What is the Spirit World Like?

Explaining the spirit world to others in terms of what it is *not* can be one of the most enlightening ways to describe it. When asked, you might say it is not a place where a clock ticks your life away, or where you have someone breathing down your neck telling you what to do, where to go and what to be. It is not a place of illness, pain or loss. Neither will your children be sent to fight wars, no one will harm you or your family and no one will enter your home to steal or cause you harm. It is a place without natural disasters, free from worry, fear and persecution. And that is just the beginning!

The earth is but a pale shadow of the greater reality beyond. A lot of the ancient illumined ones tell us we have come from the spirit world to incarnate here so that we may lead an earthly life as spirits who have human experiences as opposed to humans who have spiritual experiences. And by virtue of the after life's perfection, where else is the soul to learn the lessons? That is why the experiment called 'human beings' was created on a school of learning called the earth.

'They are Always With Me'

Our spirit friends are only with you by your consent. They are not in your shower or toilet if that is what worries you and neither are they there when you during any of your private and intimate moments (you may also be glad to know). Spiritualists described a pink colour descending over the earthly soul in order to block any intrusion. They have also put forward the idea that spirit guides act as guards in these matters. Whatever way one looks at it, *we* are the control and the things we do are known but not spied upon. Moving on from these matters, it still begs the question of just when is it they *are* with you. The truth is, they are only ever a thought away. When a loving parent sends their child into the next room to play, they have no need to see in order to know what the child is doing and whether or not they are safe.

Spiritual Etiquette

Never apply the spiritual and psychic awareness techniques herein to anyone unless so authorised by the recipient. Do not tolerate it in others. Occasionally the spirit will impinge upon you to approach a person or situation with a view to helping. In these cases you should always ask for assistance from the highest and the best. When you are acting on the part of genuine motive, the relief you can bring someone can often be described as life changing. It can be a wonderful experience to be used this way. But do not be surprised to find yourself, in a rare circumstance, rejected by the one you are trying to help.

Exacting a Fee

There is nothing wrong with charging for your services. We live in a material world and you must ensure that you and your family have enough to live on. Greed will only weaken the power of the spirit to work with you. The spiritual mantras of 'like attracts like' so attract only 'the highest and best' signify that it is not for this book to tell you where need ends and greed begins. Only you can do that.

Encountering Nature Spirits, Elementals and the Like

From time-to-time on your spiritual journey you may become aware of these special creations of the Divine. How good or bad they can be, in certain circumstances, can very much depend on you. Usually you will only become aware of them if you are in that way constituted. In these cases, follow the lead wherever it takes you. This can become a path filled with great illumination.

Humans can influence them and they can be used for good and bad.

Their role in this universe is not clearly understood as it seems they exist in an aspect of the spirit dimension dedicated to creation and maintenance, i.e. helping to fashion, form and craft the earth and everything on it in the vision of the maker. It is said they shape the baby in the womb and assist the trees of the earth to grow. They help form the rock and the mountain, the wind, the flame, the thunderbolt and the sea. They exist as separate species from each other in the same way animals, birds and mammals do. Their many forms reflect their particular function in the whole scheme of things. An example of your tangible experience of them may be as simple as empowering them to help your garden grow. They ape human behaviour and take to wearing clothes as if wishing they too were human. Their intelligence varies amongst the types, ranging from very simple to primate level. Without going into this vast area of study too deeply, your acceptance or rejection of them as real entities does not majorly impact on your development. There are numerous great workers in the field who have refused to accept many of the axioms and tenets of human psychic and spiritual awareness, and it appears not to have diminished their power to influence or realise the work of the pleroma.

The Acceptance of Things

We do not define God for others. People find God for themselves in their own unique way. We should never cast ourselves, or be cast, as intercessors in that relationship. Acceptance of wider spheres of knowledge and understanding are not prerequisites to walking the golden path of enlightenment. For example, for someone to lead a fulfilling and spiritually aware life is not dependent on them knowing all about the earth upon which they daily walk. So do not get hung up on definitions of things and laws and codes that serve only to tangle the mind. Instead, be free in what you already know and keep in mind that the more we learn, the more we realise there is to learn!

Atheists, God and The Clock in the Field

Imagine you find a clock in a field. It would be fair to assume that it did not grow there. You would have to accept that it just didn't happen by accident – the clock was made for a specific purpose. These are things we can all agree on. Take the human heart – infinitely more complex. Would it not be fair to assume, using the clock argument, that the human heart did not happen by accident? Was it not also created for a specific purpose by someone or something?

People look for God and spirit in all kinds of ways amongst the things that compose our world. Stand aside and let them search for God and spirit in our material plane for they will *never* succeed. *Why?* Because it is impossible for them to discover this proof in the trees and rocks of the earth until they are able to understand that the trees and rocks of the earth *are* the proof they seek!

We discussed earlier that Jesus never once used the word miracle. But when a cynic tells you they do not believe in miracles, you should philosophically remind them that all life is a miracle!

All is an Experiment

There is an ancient stream in Natural Spiritualism that postulates that all the work you undertake should be approached as an experiment. There are no guarantees. And that your life and the life beyond is not exempt from chance or the unknown. It is considered an error to think of 'God' as all knowing. The Gnostic texts teach that the earth itself was created as an experiment and when you become enlightened enough you will come to realise that which created you also learns from you.

Is there a way to find an answer (for certain) using psychic and spiritual awareness techniques?

There are numerous ways an answer to a perplexing question can be found. The simplest may be the pendulum.

EXERCISE
Pendulum Divination

Take a light metallic object such as a safety pin or needle and dangle it on the end of a ten inch length of natural cotton. Rest your elbow on a tabletop for steadiness with the pendulum almost an inch off the surface. Ask a control question such as, *'Is my name ... ?'* You will note the pendulum will rotate clockwise or counter clockwise. This action determines the *Yes* response. Then ask a question to which you know for sure the answer to be *No.* The pendulum should rotate in the opposite direction determining the *No* response. In certain cases it may swing north-south for one answer and east-west for the opposite response.

Now that you have a method of obtaining clear *yes* and *no* responses, you must carefully craft your questions to elicit the right reply – and herein lies the difficulty. To obtain the right answers requires the right construction of the question (or series of questions). The spirit will help you realise the specific divination of this nature and how to interpret answers gleaned from the pendulum's motion. Start simply before building up to more complex tasks and be aware that knowing the truth can be a very bitter pill to swallow. The wise among you will also allow for error in all answers obtained because the ego and human desire can sometimes override the correct action of the pendulum.

The Curse of Karma

Be careful not leave everything to karma, as so many do, thinking the universe will somehow self-correct itself. The misunderstanding of what karma actually is, acts as a dangerous and toxic mindset, leading to all manner of evil and wrongdoing being allowed to go unchecked. See it for what it is – an indoctrinated passive attitude, which was created in order to give control to the few over the many. Karma is a philosophical parasite common to all religions, albeit wrapped up as something else by the different systems, to throw followers off the scent and reinforce the dominance of their respective elites. When everything is left to karma, evil has a free hand. For evil to succeed requires only that good people do nothing! So what better device than karma to fool the world into thinking good of itself and allowing the enslavement of humanity to continue. It is an inexcusable pretext for people's tyranny. However, this is not to say there is no natural cause and effect and you are not ultimately responsible for everything you do – because you absolutely are! This rule is sewn into the very fabric of all true spiritual philosophies. The toxicity occurs when people decide, on the part of faux spirituality to, as it were, 'leave everything to karma'. Be aware of the damage done by this way of thinking.

As outlined in Chapter Two, instead of karma we have,

As you sew, so shall you reap
As you do, so you are
As you think, so shall you become!

6th Books investigates the paranormal, supernatural,
explainable or unexplainable. Titles cover everything
included within parapsychology: how to, lifestyles,
beliefs, myths, theories and memoir.